Contemporary Argumentation and Rhetoric

Michael M. Korcok
Andrea D. Thorson-Hevle

Second Edition

Kendall Hunt
publishing company

Cover image © Shutterstock, Inc. Used under license.

Kendall Hunt
publishing company

www.kendallhunt.com
Send all inquiries to:
4050 Westmark Drive
Dubuque, IA 52004-1840

Copyright © 2014 by Michael M. Korcok and Andrea D. Thorson-Hevle

ISBN 978-1-4652-6252-3

Printed in the United States of America

Contents

Introductory Concepts

Chapter Objectives

An introductory course in argumentation and rhetoric gives students the tools with which to improve their critical thinking abilities and with which to communicate that thinking in an effective manner. Effective critical thinking is necessary to understand ourselves and the world. Without effective critical thinking, we cannot make reasonable decisions about what to believe and about how to act. As individuals, our own decisions construct our lives and shape the lives of those around us. As members of family, group, community, and of the broader society and culture, our productive participation requires an ability to communicate our thinking. Together, the interplay of effective critical thinking and the ability to communicate our thoughts form the subject matter of this text.

Within this chapter, you will learn key concepts that are developed in the rest of the text. The chapter is divided into four sections. The first section discusses rhetoric, the study of persuasion and influence. The second section discusses critical thinking, the ability to form considered judgments based on evidence and good reasoning. The third section then presents arguments, including three models of argument. The final section in this chapter introduces debating on one of the formal ways that rhetoric and argumentation work in resolving disputes.

Section One	Section Two	Section Three	Section Four
• Classic Rhetoric • Contemporary Rhetoric	• The Toulmin Model • Fallacies of Logic	• The Deductive Model • The Inductive Model	• Foundations of Debate • Preparing to Debate • One-on-One Debate • Team Debate

Rhetoric

In order to understand argumentation and debate, we must first examine rhetoric. Rhetoric has enjoyed many definitions over the centuries, but there are a couple of key traits consistently found in those definitions; first, it concerns not only *what* is being said, but also *how* it is being said; second, it is persuasive in nature. Historically, philosophers, rhetoricians, and educators alike have argued the relevance of rhetoric and its relationship with logic. Many argue that rhetoric is more concerned with the stylistic devices, the *how* of the communication. Rhetoric does attend to style and delivery, but it also considers other important elements. Rhetoric also deals with meaning and symbols, persuasion and argumentation, which means it, is also about truth, logic, and reasoning. Confused? This is normal, we assure you.

Although we could offer you a simple quick definition of rhetoric and move on, doing so would only do you a disservice. Understanding what rhetoric is and how it is related to the other primary concepts discussed in this text is essential in you becoming skilled at argumentation and debate.

You may have heard people say, "that was just rhetoric." What was meant by this comment? Perhaps an accusation that what the person just said was false. This kind of comment is commonly used in describing dirty politicians, someone trying to conceal the truth, or someone perceived as using empty words. Can rhetoric be used for bad purposes? Absolutely, we are not attempting to argue that rhetoric is infallible. However, just as rhetoric is capable of being used for bad ends, it can be used for good ones. And most commonly, rhetoric is used as a means of bridging gaps in understanding and reasoning. Rhetoric is used to unite people, to motivate and inspire, it is used to persuade and reaffirm; in short, rhetoric is the root of that power that moves us towards a new goal.

Historically, rhetoric has been used to accomplish the most memorable and influential acts of our time. Consider for a moment some of the most influential speeches of all time. President Franklin D. Roosevelt's first inaugural address on March 4, 1933 was impactful, strong, and inspiring.

> "This great Nation will endure as it has endured, will revive and will prosper. So, first of all, let me assert my firm belief that the only thing we have to fear is fear itself—nameless, unreasoning, unjustified terror, which paralyzes needed efforts to convert retreat into advance. In every dark hour of our national life a leadership of frankness and vigor has met with that understanding and support of the people themselves which is essential to victory."

Roosevelt's speech, delivered in Buffalo, New York in 1883, argued that good men serve their country in government. His speech was intended to motivate and persuade his audience to take their spot in governance and do their duty.

Perhaps Martin Luther King's, *"I Have a Dream"* came to your mind. Nine out of ten students at the college and universities I teach at have immediately determined the *I Have a Dream* speech as the most memorable and famous speech in American history. Why is this? Is it that the writing of the actual speech was done impeccably? Was it the way the speaker delivered the words? Maybe it was the tones, rhythms, and persuasive passion the speaker used? Was it the literary devices? Perhaps it was the reasoning and credibility the speaker evoked? The answer is . . . this speech was a successful and memorable speech because it contained all of those components.

Martin Luther King's "I Have a Dream" speech excerpt:

> "And so even though we face the difficulties of today and tomorrow, I still have a dream. It is a dream deeply rooted in the American Dream.
>
>   I have a dream that one day this nation will rise up and live out the true meaning of its creed: "We hold these truths to be self-evident, that all men are created equal."
>
>   I have a dream that one day on the red hills of Georgia, the sons of former slaves and the sons of former slave owners will be able to sit down together at the table of brotherhood.
>
>   I have a dream that one day even the state of Mississippi, a state sweltering with the heat of injustice, sweltering with the heat of oppression, will be transformed into an oasis of freedom and justice.
>
>   I have a dream that my four little children will one day live in a nation where they will not be judged by the color of their skin but by the content of their character.
>
>   I have a dream today!"

John Locke and others have suggested that rhetoric is a powerful instrument of error and deceit. Can you recall the way you felt when you heard the *I Have a Dream* speech? Think of all the wrongs made right by that speech, all the lives saved, rights gained, and good inspired; doesn't Locke's definition seem pessimistic at best? George Campbell's definition of rhetoric would be a more accurate reflection of Martin Luther King's rhetoric. Campbell wrote, "[Rhetoric] is that art or talent by which discourse is adapted to its end. The four ends of discourse are to enlighten the understanding, please the imagination, move the passion, and influence the will." Gerard A. Hauser's definition of rhetoric is much more closely aligned to the way we use rhetoric in argumentation debate class, he states rhetoric is "an instrumental use of language." One person engages another person in an exchange of symbols to accomplish some goal. It is not communication for communication's sake. Rhetoric is communication that attempts to coordinate social action. For this reason, rhetorical communication is explicitly pragmatic. Its goal is to influence human choices on specific matters that require immediate attention."

At this point you should see the connections among these concepts. But let's review a few key concepts just to be clear. **Persuasion** is the communication that is intended to influence the acts, beliefs, values, and attitudes of others. Persuasion is used in argumentation. **Argumentation** can be understood as the communicative process of advancing, supporting, criticizing, and modifying claims so that appropriate decision makers may grant or deny adherence. **Debate** is the process of inquiry and advocacy and the seeking of a reasoned judgment on a proposition. Argumentation and persuasion are used in debate. A **discourse** can be any speech, written or spoken, and any exchange of symbols in any context, this would include newspaper, media, films, the Internet, and of course debate and argumentation. Rhetoric is the glue that binds discourse, argumentation, debate, and persuasion together. **Rhetoric** can be understood as *the art of persuasion* if you have a preference for the ancient definition. Rhetoric can also be understood as the *study of effective communication*, but for this course please refer to Campbell's definition offered above. Rhetoric and dialectic are all about how humans attempt to find truth in any given situation. Debate is the method we use in this class to come to some agreed truth. Argumentation is the mechanism or apparatus we utilize while debating to get us to that truth. By the end of this textbook, you will see more clearly how the concepts are linked.

Rhetoric has a long history and many have argued about what exactly qualifies as rhetoric, as well as who has the right to learn the art of rhetoric. While it is not possible to rehash all the details of the history of rhetoric, it is essential that we understand rhetoric's relationship to truth, power, the audience, and society. This chapter will develop a discussion on these topics and as you read future chapters the concepts herein will become clearer. Given that debate is an effort in winning an argument and coming to the best *truth*, the rhetorical contributions discussed herein are centered on the idea of truth. We will examine the historical context of rhetoric's birth and progress. It is important to note that this text is a small examination of important contributions to rhetorical theory and does not reflect the *only* significant contributions. While the contributions discussed in the following pages should be considered those most relevant to this course and those that are foundational to the understanding of debate and argumentation, they are not a fully encompassing study of the broad and complex study of rhetoric.

Critical Thinking

Defining critical thinking is a complex reflective endeavor of its own and many persons have come to conclusions about what critical thinking is and involves. For our purposes, we'll keep it simple here and define **critical thinking** as reflective reasoning used to decide what to believe and how to act. This broad understanding of what critical thinking is sets the stage for understanding its importance.

There are both practical and academic impacts of critical thinking. Making good decisions is of utmost importance in all areas of your life, both public and private. Whether it is a question of how you understand yourself and the world around you, a matter of what career to train for, which candidate to vote for, what investments to make, or who to make a life with, good critical thinking will shape your life.

That importance is recognized throughout higher education, and is probably one of the main reasons you are taking a course in argumentation and rhetoric. Taking a course or courses in critical thinking is a requirement for a bachelor's degree in the California State University system, for example. Chancellor Glenn Dumke's 1980 executive order #338 explained why:

> "Instruction in critical thinking is designed to achieve an understanding of the relationship of language to logic, which would lead to the ability to analyze, criticize, and advocate ideas, to reason inductively and deductively, and to reach factual or judgmental conclusions based on sound inferences drawn from un-ambiguous statements of knowledge or belief. The minimal competence to be expected at the successful conclusion of instruction in critical thinking should be the ability to distinguish fact from judgment, belief from knowledge, and skills in elementary inductive and deductive processes, including an understanding of the formal and informal fallacies of language and thought."

Improving critical thinking abilities occurs only by reflective use of good reasoning in everyday decisions. In order to do that, we need an understanding of and practice in reasoning well. Understanding good reasoning is accomplished by exploring the major models of argumentation developed over the years. Practice in reasoning well is accomplished by debating contemporary issues of importance to us all.

Professor Edward Glaser divided critical thinking into three areas in his 1941 development of the standard test of critical thinking ability. He noted that critical thinking is:

1. An attitude of being disposed to consider in a thoughtful way the problems and subjects that come within the range of one's experiences
2. Knowledge of the methods of logical inquiry and reasoning
3. Some skill in applying those methods.

We will work with all three of these aspects of critical thinking. We will inculcate attitudes of thoughtful deliberation in understanding difficult issues. We will introduce, explain, and apply the methods of logical inquiry and reasoning. We will develop critical thinking skills by engaging in debate.

Models of Argument

A **model** is a developed representation of something. Maps, verbal depictions, and sets of mathematical equations, for example, can be used to show us what a piece of geography, a historical event, or a physical process is. A photograph of you, for example, is not you, it is a model of you, a depiction of what you looked like at a moment of time and in a specific place. Similarly, a globe is not the Earth; it is a model of the shape and physical surface of it.

Modeling is the basic human epistemic, it is how we know. We represent the world in models and then use those models to understand the world, to act in the world, and to remake it. Human modeling has fractionated into many media and modalities for the myriad domains modeled and for the many purposes we have to model them.

Modeling serves three different but related functions in human thinking: representation, simulation, and design. The **representation** function uses models of parts of reality to describe and understand them. The **simulation** function uses models to predict how parts of the world would be like under different conditions and under varying assumptions. The **design** function creates models of things and processes for the purpose of making them actual.

An **argument** as a piece of reasoning is a set of statements, one of which serves as a conclusion, while the others together provide support for that conclusion. This definition of argument is nearly two and a half thousand years old, having been invented by Aristotle. Since critical thinking necessitates reasoning well, argumentation as reasoning is crucial to effective critical thinking. This simple definition of an argument is useful in and of itself and we will explore it in some depth shortly, but the definition hardly exhausts an understanding of what arguments are.

In our interactions with each other, we encounter arguments regularly. Whether we read them in editorials or academic journals or hear them in disputes with loved ones, or perhaps watch arguments being exchanged between political candidates, arguments are commonplace. We are expected to construct and present arguments in nearly every part of life. Whether we are engaged in selling a product or service, attempting to convince someone to see things our way or carefully considering a difficult set of ideas, there is an expectation that we will offer arguments to make our case.

To understand arguments we witness, we need to understand the models that have developed to explain them. To evaluate whether or not arguments will be successful and under which circumstances, we need to run simulations on our models of those arguments. To construct our own arguments, we need to be able to design them based on sound models of argument.

This text will present and develop three main models of argument. We will begin with the contemporary Toulmin model, the last of the models to be created. After that, we will examine the deductive model of argument, sound reasoning as understood since ancient times. We will also examine and develop the inductive model of argument: reasoning from examples and data.

Debating

Debating is organized dispute about important issues. Debates take many forms and are organized in a variety of ways, but the crux of most debates is structured disagreement about a point or matter. While debates are used by disputants as a means to advocate on behalf of beliefs, causes, and actions they believe in, that is not their most important use for our purposes. Debates are an excellent activity to develop critical thinking skills, to hone reasoning based on evidence, and to learn about argumentation and rhetoric.

Preparing to debate requires debaters to exercise their ability to research and comprehend the issues in dispute, to design and create arguments for their side of the resolution, to consider the strategic interaction of the positions they and their opponents might take, and to construct the rhetoric which will win them the debate.

In debates, the participants must listen and understand their opponents' arguments, respond to those arguments with arguments of their own, and realistically evaluate the interaction of those arguments. The need to strategically assess the relative strengths and weaknesses of the various arguments in a debate motivates debaters to consider positions fairly rather than to maintain an ideological entrenchment. Most debates privilege evidence for and against the claims at issue, and this encourages debaters to do the same.

Debates are communicative play accomplished with argument and rhetoric, with reasons and evidence, with wit and effective critical thinking. They are an excellent tool to develop those understandings and skills. This text will introduce the basics of debating and get students ready to debate well.

The effectiveness of debating in developing critical thinking skills has been the subject of numerous studies over the years. These academic studies conclude that argumentation and rhetoric courses that feature debating are an excellent way to develop students' critical thinking abilities. Dr. Winston Brembeck's doctoral dissertation in 1949, for example, found that there was a significant difference in the critical thinking gains made by students in an argumentation class compared to other students. Debate works in improving students' critical thinking.

Check Your Understanding

Explain the difference between rhetoric and argumentation

Explain the relationship between argumentation and debate

What is discourse?

Critical thinking can be divided into three parts, they are:

1.

2.

3.

What is the persuasion and how is it different or related to debate?

Explain the three functions modeling serves:

1.

2.

3.

What is George Campbell's definition of rhetoric?

What is Gerard A. Hauser's definition of rhetoric?

Explain how modeling, representation, simulation and design are relevant to the topic of rhetoric as discussed in your book.

In debate, the participants must listen to and understand their opponent's arguments, respond to those arguments with argument of their own, and do what else?

Self-Assessment: The critical thinker

1. Match opposite characteristics for the desirable traits.

   _____ enjoys arguing about politics online   a. thinks they have it all figured out
   _____ is worried their judgments are biased   b. thinks school is to get a good job
   _____ changes their mind when they're wrong   c. thinks arguing is unpleasant
   _____ considers evidence for new viewpoints   d. keeps ideas to themselves
   _____ enjoys learning about different subjects   e. goes with their gut feelings
   _____ actively seeks out data for decisions   f. doesn't think about thinking

2. Identify the most likely level of the Disagreement Hierarchy for each example.

   _____ Obamacare is bad: it's socialism with death panels.
   _____ Intelligent design is for realz, dudes. No one has proved evolution!
   _____ Climate change is real. The NASA data has Earth getting hotter over the last century.
   _____ What an angry post! Chillaxe on the meds before your next response, mkay?
   _____ He writes there's no global warming cause the oil companies fund his research.
   _____ You're a frog-licking twerp whose momma wore clownshoes to the last prom.

3. Which of the characteristics of effective critical thinking do you think is most important? Why?

   _____

   _____

   _____

   _____

4. Do you think some cultures encourage critical thinking more than others? How and why?

   _____

   _____

   _____

   _____

CHAPTER

2 Classical Rhetoric

Chapter Objectives

Classical rhetoric is the foundation upon which both argumentation and rhetoric stand. Rhetoric has been part of the academic training of educated persons for thousands of years: it is one of the most ancient academic fields. In medieval Europe, for example, rhetoric, grammar, and logic formed the *Trivium*, the subjects students were taught first. Argumentation was born, via Aristotle, from rhetoric.

Within this chapter, you will learn the major concepts of classical rhetoric. The chapter develops the subject historically, examining the ideas of major thinkers, with a focus on the ideas of Aristotle. In this chapter you will learn:

1. where and when the study of rhetoric began
2. how rhetoric was defined and regarded during Classical times.
3. the major contributions of Aristotle.

The Beginning: Corax and Sophists

A man named Corax in 465 B.C.E. at the Greek colony of Syracuse, Sicily created the first recorded written rhetoric in our Western world. During this time the government had undergone a change and land disputes were rampant. Corax came to realize that the person who was able to dispute their side best would ultimately be the "winner" or owner of the land. Therefore, it seemed that power resided in the person who could plead the more plausible, logical, and overall effective case. Given this realization, Corax created a system of argumentation that would lead people to win their cases and thus their land. Corax's theory on argumentation and rhetoric soon spread to Athens and many other cities.

In Athens, citizens spoke for themselves; there was not the legal form of refutation we are familiar with today in terms of legal representation. This meant each citizen's probability of winning their case relied greatly on the quality of their speech and the delivery of their arguments. The wealthier families were able to pay for speechwriters to help them construct arguments, as well as to have access to the best educators. In short, they were able to higher today's version of lawyers or consultants. Until Corax, the ability for the average citizen to have access to quality argumentation was all but impossible.

In 490 B.C.E., a group of educators traveled city by city offering educational courses to citizens for a price. These roaming educators were called **Sophists**. Their goal was to make their students into *good* citizens. In their teachings, they emphasized forms of persuasive expression, such as the art of rhetoric, which provided pupils with skills useful for achieving success in life, particularly public life. Although rhetoric was taught often, Sophists also taught subjects like grammar and art.

At the time, access to education was a privilege afforded to those with birthright. In contrast, primarily, the Sophist educators of the time, sought to educate those who could pay for their services—regardless of their status in society. This approach angered many aristocracies. The Sophists did not make education available to all citizens, but they did educate a great many people who without their teachings would never have had access to such an education. Unlike other educators at the time, the Sophists centered their teachings purely on usable knowledge, that is, knowledge that citizens could use in the social and political realms of their everyday lives, and thus it was highly useful and advantageous to acquire.

The Sophists also taught a delivery style that enhanced the language. Their delivery was engaging and performance-like. Delivery was taught as a central element of rhetoric, not cast aside as an unimportant consideration like so many other teachers of this time. Fundamentally, the Sophists did not claim that they had an ultimate truth or that they could teach someone to come to know the truth of something. Instead, they claimed that rhetoric helps us see the reality the speaker tries to create through language and they could help others craft useful rhetoric. The rhetoric the Sophists disseminated focused on practicality—how could this be useful in real life—instead of on the philosophical theory. The focus on delivery was a primary reason Plato criticized the Sophists, Plato claimed the Sophists were teaching mere flattery[1]. He did not like that Sophists because he did not focus on absolute truth, he did not like that they focused on delivery, and he did not like that they offered teaching of this art to people who normally would not have had access to it.

Given that political careers were the most popular ambitions at the time, the Sophists spent much, if not most, of their time teaching rhetoric. Politicians from distant cities would come to take in a lecture from the famous Sophists in an attempt to increase their ability to present arguments effectively. Perhaps one of the most controversial and notable beliefs these first teachers of rhetoric held was their disinterest in absolute truth; they did not believe in an absolute truth, only **probable truth**. Traditionally, society had valued the idea of coming to the "real" truth of matters, not to the best argued position.

The Sophists were relativists. **Relativism** is the idea that "truth" is not an absolute; rather, it is relative to the person or persons who hold the belief in question. Relativists, like the Sophists, believed humans are incapable of achieving absolute truth because the nature of the mind is limited. They also believed that understanding the power of language is crucial to the exploration of knowledge and is an essential tool to harness, control, and apply. Unlike others of the time, Sophists humanized philosophy. Before the Sophists, philosophy was often formulaic and prescriptive; by putting the person at the center of the argument process, the Sophists added a new component to the philosophy. Unlike Plato, who will be discussed later, the Sophists were not concerned with arriving at the ultimate "truth"; rather, they were interested in teaching people how to win an argument. They created a series of arguments that they claimed would always win. The Sophists controversially asserted that a person need not know an area well in order to defend or refute it; you must merely have the right rhetoric. Some of their techniques include manipulations, entrapping their opponents, large fiery language to intimidate, and even attempts to confuse, but they also used elements of logic and reasoning. Clearly, the Sophists did not always teach rhetoric from the most moral standpoint, which would ultimately lead to their demise.

The Sophists taught their students to examine multiple sides of a given issue and deal in probabilities based on knowledge. Some, like Plato, criticized the fact that Sophists did not believe in a nominal world where transcendent forms of knowledge and truth exist, but rather focused more sharply on existential realities.[2] The divergence in both sides' views of rhetoric can be summarized as a contention between existentialism and transcendence. **Existentialism** can be understood as a philosophical approach that highlights the existence of a person as a free entity who determines their own development.

---

[1]Plato, Gorgias, trans. By W.R.M Lamb Cambridge, Massachusetts: Harvard Univeristy Press, 1967, passim
[2]Plato, Gorgias, trans. By W.R.M Lamb Cambridge, Massachusetts: Harvard Univeristy Press, 1967, passim

Figure 2.1 Corith, Greece.

The Sophists believed rhetoric was good for civic virtue—the training of people to be good citizens.[3] They also felt strongly that humans control their own destiny. Major criticisms of the Sophists were that they were naive relativists—that they believed that knowledge is relative to the limited nature of the mind and the conditions of knowing. They taught the use of language to create illusions to convince an audience, instead of using rhetoric to uncover illusions.

The period from 50 A.D. through 400 A.D. became known as the Second Sophistic, a time that marked the transition from the classical to the British period of rhetorical history. The Second Sophistic was a period that concentrated on the delivery and style of speech and less on the actual subject matter. It was a time where rhetoric became an "art of giving effectiveness to the speaker." It was a time that marked the final years of the Roman Empire, which was known for great political unrest. Oratorical and rhetorical theory had to adapt to the political and social style and delivery that were appropriate to this new time.

Although some contended that the Sophists were not educators, but money-hungry men teaching others how to manipulate and deceive; it is important to note, that although they were not centered on what was right or wrong, they did teach people the basic tools of argumentation, which became the groundwork for other philosophers and rhetoricians like Aristotle. Sophists also provided education to people who did not have access to those particular arts before. Perhaps most significantly, the Sophists illustrated the usefulness and advantage of passionate delivery.

Plato

One could not discuss important contributions in rhetorical theory regarding truth without mentioning two key players: Plato and Aristotle. Contrary to the Sophists, Plato was primarily concerned with arriving at a given truth of a situation or issue. You may have heard instructors, or others, discuss "ultimate truths." This concept comes from Plato's obsession with discovering what is termed the *ultimate truth*.

---

[3]http://www.oxforddictionaries.com/us/definition/american_english/existentialism

The Sophists were not concerned with whether the side they argued was correct; rather, they focused on the goal of getting others to accept the speaker's position. Plato, on the other hand, sought to find the absolute truth in a given situation and believed that the ethical use of rhetoric could aid in the discovery of truth. Plato argued that people like the sophists taught and used **false rhetoric** for the pursuit of personal interests over the interest of finding ultimate truth.

In today's world you could compare the idea of "false rhetoric" to a car salesperson. A family needs a car and a salesperson helps them find one. The family needed a car so they benefited from the sale, but the salesman also benefited. In Plato's sense of rhetoric, both the customer and salesperson should try to arrive at the ultimate truth regarding the worth of the car (as if there were a universal and perfect truth for a car). Naturally, the person buying the car does not want to spend any more than necessary—even if spending less might hurt the salesperson's income. Do not forget the salesperson also has personal motives to sell the vehicle (money and sales for the month). The salesperson will sell the car at a price that may not be the true worth of the vehicle because it would benefit them to do so. Therefore, both people are trying to persuade the other to accept a specific price for the car—even if the offer is not the "true" worth of the car, and with no effort to "discover" the actual, true worth of the car. Plato would call this **false rhetoric** because it would not lead to the ultimate truth (the worth of the car). In the end, the better persuader or arguer will win this argument, which really means the Sophistic method will win out. The buyers will walk away with their great deal or be smoked by the salesperson, but no "truth" will be revealed. Plato feels rhetoric should be used to unveil truth, not as a means to deceive or just persuade.

Plato's concern with "ultimate" or "transcendent" truth led him to believe that before humans are born their souls exist in a place that has access to absolute truths. When humans are born, they forget the truths their souls had once absorbed. Plato believed that now, in order for humans to arrive at truth, a series of questions, or rather the correct question(s), must be asked. We use this idea nowadays, when we use a series of questions to arrive at "truth" in our courts of law, or even when a loved one comes home far too late one night and you bombard them with questions to arrive at the truth of where they were.

Initially, Plato claimed that rhetoric was not a means of arriving at truth. Rather, he believed rhetoric was audience centered, concerned with persuasion, and not always a virtuous endeavor. Eventually, Plato did come to appreciate rhetoric and acknowledge that rhetoric has the power to produce knowledge, but stressed that rhetoric can only provide ways of *conveying* truth. Plato believed that in order to arrive at ultimate truth, one must engage in dialectic. **Dialectic** would allow humans to separate the truth from the false through questioning. His dialogues, *Gorgias* and

Figure 2.2 Plato founded the Academy in Athens, the first known institution of higher learning in the Western World. He was a noted philosopher, writing thirty-six dialogues, many of which were devoted to the subject of rhetoric.

Phaedrus, discussed false and true rhetoric in depth. Socrates, a character in Plato's dialogues, argues that human souls exist with the "form of the good" which refers to justice and knowledge. For a true and full understanding of Plato and these ideas you should consult his primary works. Generally, Plato disagreed with the Sophistic notion that an art of persuasion (rhetoric) can exist apart from dialectic, claiming that the Sophists appeal only to the probable rather than to that which is true. In the end, Plato argued that Sophists did not focus on bettering the audience, but flattering them.

Plato's *Gorgias* focused on the idea of false rhetoric. Plato's primary purpose was to use two characters in a debate to show the flaws in the ideas of the main character, Gorgias. Gorgias was a famous Sicilian sophist who introduced probability-based argumentation. Plato uses the arguments progressed by Gorgias as an opportunity to dismantle the ideas he asserted. The character he used to dismantle these arguments was Socrates. One of Socrates' primary arguments was that rhetoric was not an art. One of the more famous accusations in the *Gorgias* is when Socrates professes that rhetoric is a form of "cookery". Cookery in today's terms would mean something that was cooked up or contrived; it lacks real substance, something that is fake, selfish, and performance based. Plato's *Phaedrus* focuses on "true rhetoric."[1] This work employs an allegory to discuss the art of speaking. This time, the main idea of the dialogue focuses on what is good and true rhetoric, unlike the *Gorgias* which focuses on deliberating what is false or bad rhetoric. Plato asserts the ideal speaker is one who is moral and truthful[4].

According to Plato, rhetoric is, "A kind of influencing of the mind by means of persuasion." Plato considered rhetoric to be a psychological form, believing that one can only be truly healthy if one understands how the mind responds to various persuasions. He discussed the idea of adapting to audiences based on various criteria. He specifically discussed sex, area of residence, and age. The most common definition of rhetoric attributed to Plato is rhetoric as the "art of winning the soul by discourse."

He believed that men and women should be appealed to through similar means when he stated, "There is no special faculty of administration in a state which a woman has because she is a woman, or which a man has by virtue of his sex, but the gifts of nature are alike diffused in both; all the pursuits of men are the pursuits of women.[5]" Plato spent much time on the thought of persuasion by means of the mind, but his student, Aristotle, would spend even more time deciphering the links among rhetoric, persuasion, dialectic, and the mind. He warned that young audiences are usually unable to grasp more complex ideas and are overly concerned with the way they are perceived by others[6].

Other Famous Quotes Commonly Attributed to Plato

1. "Wise men speak because they have something to say; Fools because they have to say something."
2. "People are like dirt. They can either nourish you and help you grow as a person or they can stunt your growth and make you wilt and die."

---

[4]Plato, Gorgias, trans. 1967
[5]Jowett, Plato's Republic p. 179.
[6]The Rhetoric of Western Thought. James L. Golden, Goodwin F. Berquist, William E. Coleman

Aristotle

Aristotle synthesized two polarizations set forth by the Sophistic and Platonic worldviews. It was the intersection of these two paradigms that inspired the work of one of the most influential thinkers in the history of philosophy. Aristotle has long been considered the most distinguished student of Plato and the greatest contributor to rhetorical theory and analysis. The Sophistic notion that rhetoric was an art helped inspire Aristotle's famous argument of "audience adaptation." Aristotle was more enthusiastic about rhetoric than Plato and developed two definitions. The first is "Rhetoric is the counterpart of dialectic." The second definition offered by Aristotle is, "So let rhetoric be defined as the faculty of discovering in the particular case what are the available means of persuasion." Many theorists today still struggle with interpreting Aristotle's words, especially in this last definition. However, from what we understand and can interpret, Aristotle deems persuasion as an essential part of the rhetorical process and views rhetoric as a moral and practical art. The most common definition of rhetoric attributed to Aristotle is rhetoric is "the faculty of discovering in any particular case all the available means of persuasion."

Aristotle classified discourse into three areas. First, he had **forensic** discourse. This discourse dealt with the past and criminality, such as, in a court of law. Second, **epideictic**, dealt with blame and praise; what you might hear at a special occasion like a funeral or a dedication. The third form was **deliberative**, which dealt with future policy and will be a primary focus of this text. Deliberative discourse has been one of the main focuses of American academic debate since the mid 1920's. Regardless of which you use, Aristotle contended that there needed to be four parts to any discourse: an introduction, clear statement, an argument, and a conclusion.

He specialized in observing all things living and nonliving and in formulating the data from his observations in a form that others could then study and practice. His specialties were not limited to merely the sciences, but also encompassed law, drama, and ethics. While Plato believed in transcendent truth, Aristotle was more concerned with **empirical truth**. Aristotle believed logic and scientific demonstration allow humans to arrive at truth, asserting rhetoric should be a more pragmatic endeavor than that articulated by Plato. In contrast to his teacher Plato, Aristotle believed rhetoric was the counterpart of dialectic.

Figure 2.3 A famous Greek philosopher, Aristotle is best known for contributing the canons and proofs to the field of rhetoric. Aristotle established the library of Lyceum, was the pupil of Plato, taught Alexander the Great and published numerous books.

© Panos Karas, 2014. Used under license from Shutterstock, Inc.

---

[7]As qutd. in. Goldmen, Berquist, Goodmen; 2000, p. 30

In this belief, Aristotle admits dialectical methods are necessary to find truth in theoretical discussion, but rhetorical methods should be used to find truth in practical experiences (legal conditions such as in a court of law). Aristotle articulated four distinct reasons for studying, practicing, and understanding rhetoric[7]:

1. To uphold truth and justice and play down their opposites
2. To teach in a way suitable to a popular audience
3. To analyze both sides of a question
4. To enable one to defend oneself

Proofs: Ethos, Pathos, and Logos

One of the elements to persuasion, according to Aristotle, are proofs, which he terms **ethos, pathos, and logos**. Aristotle claimed that you could support and defend your ideas with these proofs. **Ethos** is described as those proofs that depend on the speaker's ability to be believable. **Pathos** are proofs designed to affect a listener's feelings. **Logos** uses reasoning to convince the hearers. "Of the modes of persuasion furnished by the spoken word there are three kinds. The first kind depends on the personal character of the speaker; the second on putting the audience into a certain frame of mind; the third on the proof, or apparent proof, provided by the words of the speech itself.[8]"

Ethos

"Persuasion is achieved by the speaker's personal character when the speech is so spoken as to make us think [them] credible. We believe good [people] more fully and more readily than others: this is true generally whatever the question is, and absolutely true where exact certainty is impossible and opinions are divided ... [the speakers] character may almost be called the most effective means of persuasion he possesses.[9]"

Ethos is an appeal to the audience's sense of honesty and character. Ethos is how the rhetoric convinces the audience that the speakers are credible and qualified to speak on the subject as well as convince the audience that they have good intentions towards them. Aristotle believed that ethos comprised three main things: good will, good sense, and credibility (intelligence and virtue).

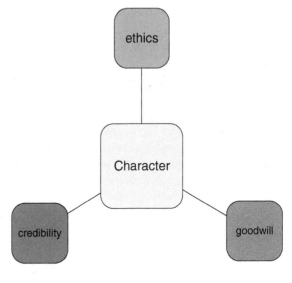

Ethos is created by the rhetor, displayed in the message, and dependent on the audience's perception of the character of the rhetor. For Aristotle, ethos was central to the speaker's persuasive potential. He believed ethos should be generated during the course of a speech and not be based on a previous reputation with

[8]Aristotle. On Rhetoric: A Theory of Civic Discourse. Trans. George A. Kennedy. 2nd ed. New York: Oxford University, 2007. Print. 1356b
[9]Aristotle, Rhetoric 1.2.1356a.4–12
[10]Aristotle, Rhetoric

the audience (1356)[10]. Today, however, when we discuss ethos we recognize both the speaker's perceived character during the speech and the speaker's credibility *before* the speech as well.

Before we can expect to convince an audience we must first be seen as a credible speaker in the eyes of the audience. When people are convinced that a speaker is knowledgeable, trustworthy, and has their best interests at heart they will be more likely to believe the speaker and accept and even act on their arguments. Keep in mind, ethos reflects the audience's perceptions of a speaker, not necessarily the "truth" of the speaker's credibility. So, then, how exactly do we manage to be perceived as credible? There are many aspects to creating your ethos as a speaker. Aristotle first articulated these ideas and we still use them today. Rhetors should ask themselves:

> Does the audience believe I am a good person with good intentions?
> Do they think I am a person of authority on the topic?
> Do they think I am honest and good-natured?

Pathos

Persuasion may come through the hearers,
when the speech stirs their emotions.[11]"

Aristotle felt a study of emotion was essential to the systematic process of public speaking. He asserted **pathos** was "putting the audience in the right frame of mind," arguing that pathos was the component of speech that affects judgment and stimulates the emotions (as qutd. in Herrick, 2005, p. 83). There are methods speakers can be taught in an effort to enhance the likelihood pathos attempts will work; however, Aristotle also warns us that that the power to get your audience to receive your ideas by playing to their emotions like pity, fear, pain, and hostility can become unethical if your efforts result in a audience left unaware of potential harms and consequences. The corruption of an audience for one's own personal gain is not a virtuous act and should be avoided.

Pathos is the Greek word for "suffering" and "experience." When speakers use pathos they are attempting to inspire empathy or an emotional response, in hopes of changing attitudes, behaviors, and/or beliefs. In simple terms, pathos, is the speakers appeal to the audience's emotions. Speakers use pathos when they want to make the audience feel what the speaker wants them to feel. Pathos is the artistic, expressive, passionate layer of a given speech. It is the moment(s) of a speech in which the speaker attempts to move the audience to action, to inspire, to motivate, to create an emotional climate amongst his/her listeners.

Classical Figures of Speech Used to Increase Pathos

adhortatio: A commandment, promise, or exhortation intended to move one's consent or desires.
adynaton: The expression of the inability of expression—almost always emotional in its nature.
aganactesis: An exclamation proceeding from deep indignation.
apagoresis: A statement designed to inhibit someone from doing something.
aposiopesis: Breaking off suddenly in the middle of speaking, usually to portray being overcome with emotion.

---

[11]ARISTOTLE, "Rhetoric", 350 BCE

apostrophe: Turning one's speech from one audience to another, or addressing oneself to an abstraction or the absent—almost always as a way of increasing appeal through emotion.

cataplexis: Threatening/prophesying payback for ill-doing.

conduplicatio: The repetition of a word or words in adjacent phrases or clauses, either to amplify the thought or to express emotion.

deesis: The vehement expression of desire put in terms of "for someone's sake" or "for God's sake."

descriptio: Vivid description, especially of the consequences of an act, that stirs up its hearers.

diacope: Repetition of a word with one or more between, usually to express deep feeling.

ecphonesis: An emotional exclamation.

enargia: Enargia, or vivid description, can be inherently moving, especially when depicting things graphic in nature.

epimone: Persistent repetition of the same plea in much the same words, a direct method for underscoring the pathetic appeal.

epitrope: A figure in which one turns things over to one's hearers (often pathetically).

"persuasion is effected through the speech itselfwhen we have proved a truth or an apparent truth by meansof the persuasive arguments suitable to the case in question12."

Logos refers to the appeal to logic. Logic is a rhetor's ability to present solid and rational reasoning on a given matter to a given audience. This was Aristotle's most stressed of the three proofs, yet logos alone will not win an argument; all the proofs are important.

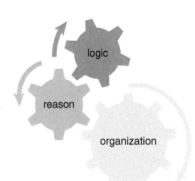

Logos can be divided into inductive and deductive logic. Logos means "word" in Greek and is primarily concerned with the consistency of the rhetor's message, the clarity of their logic, reasoning, and claims. Deductive and indicative logic as well as syllogisms and enthymemes are primary components of this proof, which will be discussed in depth in upcoming chapters. In the meantime, you can absorb the idea that logos is an appeal to an audience's sense of reasoning. This is usually accomplished through reasoned argumentation, analysis, and evidence.

Famous Quotes Commonly Attributed to Aristotle

"It is the mark of an educated mind to be able to entertain a thought without accepting it."
"Love is composed of a single soul inhabiting two bodies."
"We are what we repeatedly do. Excellence, then, is not an act, but a habit."

Aristotle's Five Canons of Rhetoric

Aristotle also contributed to what is now termed the five canons of rhetoric: invention, arrangement, style, memory, and delivery. Rhetoric was divided into these categories and is currently the most accepted template for rhetorical education and pedagogy. Rhetorical treatises through the centuries have been drawn from these categories. At different points in time different areas were considered more important than others. For instance, at first delivery was not considered as important, but some time later rhetoric was almost purely defined as style and delivery. Now rhetoricians accept all areas as equally important and recognize the importance of having each one in a given rhetorical act. We will briefly touch on the five areas, dedicating considerably more effort to areas like delivery and style because other canons, such as invention and arrangement, will be given significant attention in the coming chapters.

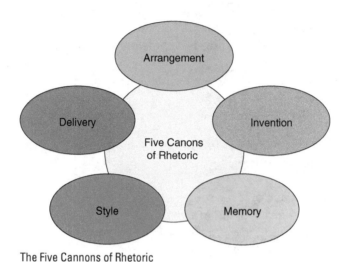

The Five Cannons of Rhetoric

Introduction	• the start of a speech, where the orator announces the subject, purpose, and persuasion in an attempt to gain credibility.
Statement of facts	• the speaker provides a narrative of what the current situation is and explains the nature of the case including a summary of the issues and/or a statement of the charge.
Division	• the speaker outlines what will come and reviews what has been said, or the point at issue in the case. This can be easily understood as a preview and review of points and basic organizational structure.
The proof	• this is where the speaker appeals to logic and rationality.
Refutation	• is where the speaker answers the counterarguments of her/his opponent.
Conclusion	• is the summary of the issue and main points and conventionally includes an appeal to pathos.

Invention

Invention is concerned with *what* is said rather than *how* it is said; thus invention is associated closely with the rhetorical appeal of logos (discussed in chapter two). Invention comes from the Latin word *"invenire,"* which means "to find," because the first step in the rhetorical process is to find the persuasive argument. *Topoi* (a Greek term meaning places) or "topics of invention" were created to help brainstorm for ideas.

Topoi are the basic categories of relationships among ideas and they serve as simple templates for creating the foundation to your arguments. Aristotle divided these *topois* or topics into two categories: common and special. Common topics include: definition, division, comparison, relationship, circumstances, testimony, notion, and conjugates. The special topics include: judicial (justice vs. injustice), deliberative (good, unworthy, advantages, disadvantages), and ceremonial (virtue and vice). These concepts are expanded in the remainder of this text.

Arrangement

Arrangement dictates how a speech or writing should be organized. Originally, in ancient rhetoric, arrangement was concerned only with oration, now we have broadened rhetoric to include the written form as well. When you learn about formal debate in the coming chapters you will be taught the various arrangements that are ideal for each type of debate and debate speech. The **classical** arrangement of oration is:

Style

Style is the artful expression of ideas. There are seven pure types of style: clarity, grandeur, beauty, rapidity, character, sincerity, and force. Style is concerned with how something is said. Style is meant to align the appropriate verbal expression for the orator's given intentions. Two of Aristotle's students, Theophrastus and Demetrius, originally developed "virtues" of style. The rules are quite simple, but very necessary. For instance, one virtue is correctness. **Correctness** refers to the idea that a speaker/writer must adhere to the specific and complete grammar and syntax rules. The speaker must employ good and competent **language** as well. In short, the speaker must display high ethos through the use of impressive language. The speaker must also be **clear and simple**. It its essential one's audience understand the message if they are to be persuaded by it. This virtue of style stresses the importance of clarity over complexity.

Evidence is the next virtue of style. Evidence is not like the supporting evidence used in court cases or scholarly journals used to reinforce an argument. In its original form, evidence referred to the use of effective pathos as accomplished primarily through vivid language. Evidence, otherwise known today as vivid language, is language that is colorful, concrete, and appeals to the senses. Vivid language

Figure 2.4 Stylistic evidence is the vivid, textured, artful expression of ideas that produce images in the mind of your audience.

choices help paint a picture in the mind of the audience. As the artist (speaker) your brushes and color palette are the tools with which you construct your argument, imagery, and purpose. The audience should be able to feel and see what the speaker is saying and vivid language choices are a great way to accomplish that task.

The next virtue, although common sense like the others, is too often ignored these days and that is the virtue of **propriety**. The term propriety seems like a term out of a 1950's family film, but it really is important still today. The virtue of **propriety** is basically the idea that speakers must be cognizant of what is appropriate given the occasion, audience, and timing.

And the final virtue, but certainly not the least important virtue, is called ornateness. **Ornateness** is a fancy way of saying the speech needs to be pleasant and interesting and it needs to manage to maintain the audience's attention. This is accomplished through the use of tonal variation of the speaker's voice, ensuring the rhythm of the speech is

Figure 2.5 Good speechmaking will encompass many varying tonal changes. Monotone speakers cause their audience to loose interest and sometimes no amount of logos can bring them back.

pleasing and diverse enough to keep the audience interested, as well as the use of various figures of speech. Below you will find a quick table of several figures of speech used today; this list is certainly not complete, as there are a great number of figures of speech a rhetor could choose. Classical rhetoric divided figures of speech into **tropes** (changes in the meaning of words) and **schemes** (changes in the pattern of words).

Memory

The degree to which an orator remembers their speech is the primary understanding of memory. Memory as a canon also considers the methods a speaker uses to ensure the audience retains the speech's primary teachings and persuasions. Mary Carruthers (1990) states, "To help recall something we have heard rather than seen, we should attach to their words the appearance, facial expression, and gestures of the person speaking as well as the appearance of the room. The speaker should therefore create strong visual images, through expression and gesture, which will fix the impression of his words. All the rhetorical textbooks contain detailed advice on declamatory gesture and expression; this underscores the insistence of Aristotle, Avicenna, and other philosophers, on the primacy and security for memory of the visual over all other sensory modes, auditory, tactile, and the rest (p. 94–95). One of the most well known for their focus on memory was a famous Greek poet, Simonides of Ceos, who declared that should anyone want to train their memory they must

Figure 2.6 Memory is a cannon in which an orator recalls their speech. There are many techniques speakers use to aid help them store their speech information. How will you store your information?

"select places and form mental images of the things they wish to remember and store those images in the places, so that the order of the places will preserve the order of the things, and the images of the things will denote the things themselves, and we shall employ the places and the images respectively as a wax writing tablet the letters written upon it."[12]

Delivery

Delivery is essential to appealing to the audience's emotions (pathos) and is critical in establishing a speaker's credibility (ethos). Delivery deals primarily with verbal utterances and emotional impact but with also body language, gestures, and tonal fluctuations. Because this canon is especially important to understanding the mastery of rhetoric as an art, we have discussed it in greater detail below. Delivery in the Classical Era is much the same as today's understanding. Movement, body, face, and voice are all components the canon of delivery centered on long ago and it is still important today. We have managed over the years to dedicate more specific examination of the delivery canon that is useful.

The canons of rhetoric are each important and even critical to debate and persuasion in general. In the text thus far and in the coming chapters we will have examined the canons of arrangement and invention significantly. Much of this text focuses on building credibility (ethos) and logic (logos) within your argument construction, but delivery (an essential skill to pathos and ethos) is of substantial importance as well and should not be overlooked when you are practicing your speeches and participating in debate. We will explore the importance of and the role of delivery in speechmaking, argumentation, and debate in this section.

Much of the population thinks communicating effectively is a formula of words and sequence. However, effective communication means making sure one's body language and tone of voice are consistent with the content of the speech. Tone, volume, and inflection make up 38% of communication (Berkley, 1999). Tone can add "music" to a speech, affect selling ability, and thrust an audience towards expressing a full continuum of emotions.

Delivery has been considered an integral part of communication, argumentation, and debate for centuries. Hellenistic and Roman treaties gave delivery significant deliberation. Aristotle wrote that delivery "is of the greatest importance . . . it is a manner of voice . . . used for each emotion" (*Rhetoric* 1403b20; Johnstone, 2001). Aristotelian thought considers the following in terms of delivery: manner of presentation, mode of presentation (impromptu, extemporaneous, memory, and manuscript), body language, posture, gestures, movement, eye contact, vocal skills including articulation, and ultimately how the physical characteristics of a given rhetor affect the audience.

The Sophists, Cicero, Quintilian, and even Plato dedicated much of their discussion on rhetoric to the concept of delivery. In the 4th and 5th centuries, the Sophists taught the importance of eliciting emotional change in the audience partly through one's acoustic control (Golden, Berquist, & Coleman 2000; Johnstone 2001; Hikins 1996). Cicero claimed delivery was the most important skill a rhetor could ever possess. "A moderate speaker with a trained delivery can often out do the best of them" (Cicero, III.11.19; Johnstone, 2001, p. 124). Quintilian agreed, saying, "A mediocre speech supported by all the power of delivery will be more impressive than the best speech unaccompanied by such power" (XI.3.5-6; Johnstone, 2001, p. 124).

---

[12] Cicero, De oratore, II, lxxxvi, 351-4, English translation by E.W. Sutton and H. Rackham from Loeb Classics Edition

Delivery includes verbal and nonverbal elements. The major components of delivery that you need to be aware of and master in order to be a fully effective rhetor, arguer, or debater are: articulation, enunciation, pronunciation, tone, pitch, speech rate, pausing, expressions, and eye contact. For a more rounded and full understanding of how to master the art of delivery you should consider taking a public speaking course.

Someone who articulates well is a speaker who puts words together well and is able to convey meaning in a clear, straightforward yet, relatively sophisticated and educated manner. **Articulation** has components of enunciation and pronunciation. Generally, articulation reflects the speaker's credibility, perceived level of intelligence, and vocabulary.

Enunciation is the manner of speaking clearly and concisely. Speech and debate instructors often give their students a series of exercises to ensure they utter the sounds of each letter in a clear and precise manner in order to better their enunciation. The opposite of good enunciation is mumbling or slurring.

Pronunciation is a part of enunciation and therefore articulation. Pronunciation is to pronounce the sounds of words correctly. Various cultures pronounce words differently. For instance you may have heard people refer to "tomatoe versus tomahtoe"—it is the same word, just pronounced differently within different dialects. You want to try to use the dialect of your audience or at least be aware that if your dialect is different you risk misunderstandings.

Tone on the other hand is not as easily described, as its qualities are difficult to define. Tone incorporates subtle cues of the rhetor's attitude, emotions, and persuasive efforts understood as "the quality of voice." Given this, the quality of delivery in the utterance of words can significantly amplify or distort the purpose or rhetorical attempts of a given speech. Tone displays a wide range of emotions, energies, and descriptors. It carries social information, such as in a sarcastic, condescending, or subservient manner of speaking. Tone adds meaning and emotion to actual chosen words. Although tone is often identified with the implied or underlying meaning of a word, tone is much more subtle and delicate and occurs with the actual vocal control of the speaker. Tone has the unique ability to capture the essence of emotion that other forms of language cannot.

Your topic or your subject determines much of your tone. If you are giving the formal introduction of a renowned individual at a conference, it is quite possible that your speech will be formal and your tone serious yet inspired. Your tone is going to be quite different in a speech congratulating the graduating class than if you are giving the eulogy at a funeral. Tone can convey hopefulness, sadness, regret, deep intrigue, and light and airy kindness. Given the proper commitment, practice, and authenticity you can manage just about any tone you like in a speech.

To improve the accuracy of your tone consider the following:

1. Breathing from the diaphragm
2. Keeping vocal cords moist with water the day of a speech
3. Practicing lower tones in the most pathos-oriented parts of your speech
4. Practicing the same paragraphs with different tones

Pitch refers to the highness or lowness of the utterance itself, specifically, level, range, and variation. The pitch variation is very important. I'm sure you can recall a moment when you listened to someone speak with an annoying pitch and, although you may have tried to look interested, you heard absolutely nothing of what they had to say. Pitch cannot be underrated.

Rate refers to the speed at which the rhetor speaks. It can also be understood as the number of words spoken per minute. A speaker's rate of speech often increases when she/he is nervous. A fast rate of speech will signal to the audience that you lack confidence and are weak, unsettled, insecure, and incompetent. None of these perceptions are necessarily accurate, but the accuracy is unimportant, the perception is what matters. Be sure to control your breathing; do not run out of air when you speak, take moments that draw out your point by delivering it slowly and with a low tone and then add a quickened pace for diversity and interest. **Pauses** are essential tools in speaking, pauses are intervals of silence between or within words, phrases, or sentences what add meaning, create drama, reflect emotion, and more. When pauses are planned they can create a great sense of movement and emotional display.

Movement includes the physical shifts in the speaker's body, whether that be through actual purposefully planned steps and shifts of weight or more distracting negative speaker behaviors such as swaying back and forth, kicking or shaking legs, shifting back and forth, nervous habits, etc. A speaker with confident powerful movements will win the audience's attention; as we know, gaining the attention of an audience is not always a simple task. Fail to move with confidence and your audience will surely divert their attention elsewhere. An amazing message is worthless if it is never truly heard. Gestures and facial expressions are valuable traits of a skilled speaker. Movements in eyebrows, corners of the lips, and even the range of gestures can make all the difference.

Similarly, **posture** refers to the relative relaxation or rigidity and vertical position of the body. A rigid speaker who lacks natural stance and gesture will reflect a lack of professionalism, preparation, and general credibility. You are always being judged when you are a speaker, your posture communicates to your audience whether or not you are credible and whether they should bother paying attention to you. The great orators and rhetors employed impeccable posture while they delivered their messages.

Cicero and Quintilian

Quintilian was a teacher and writer who composed major works on the art of oratory. He made significant contributions to educational theory, crisis theory, and rhetoric. He was the pupil of Domitius Afer and participated in the legal courts, which is in part why his contribution to rhetoric merges advocacy so greatly. His most famous book, *Institutio Oratoria*, was first published in Rome around 95 A.D. Quintilian taught that a great rhetorician must be a moral human and also possess and practice the skills of oratory.

Figure 2.7 Stack of works by famous Greek Philosophers.

© Panos Karas, 2014. Used under license from Shutterstock, Inc.

"The first question which confronts us is "What is rhetoric?" Many definitions have been given; but the problem is really twofold. For the dispute turns either on the quality of the thing itself or on the meaning of the words in which it is defined. The first and chief disagreement on the subject is found in the fact that some think that even bad men may be called orators, while others, of whom I am one, restrict the name of orator and the art itself to those who are good. Of those who divorce eloquence from that yet fairer and more desirable title to renown, a virtuous life, some call rhetoric merely a power, some a science, but not a virtue, some a practice, some an art, though they will not allow the art to have anything in common with science or virtue, while some again call it a perversion of art or κακοτεχυία.[13]

For my part, I have undertaken the task of molding the ideal orator, and as my first desire is that he should be a good man, I will return to those who have sounder opinions on the subject. Some however identify rhetoric with politics, Cicero calls it a *department of the science of politics* (and science of politics and philosophy are identical terms), while others again call it a *branch of philosophy*, among them Isocrates. The definition which best suits its real character is that which makes rhetoric the *science of speaking well.* For this definition includes all the virtues of oratory and the character of the orator as well, since no man can speak well who is not good himself."[14]

Cicero is most remembered for his contribution to the canons of rhetoric and his work *In De Inventione.* Between Cicero and Quintilian, Romans quickly became masters of rhetoric. They taught the proofs that Aristotle invented and particularly liked the appeal to logos. They did, however, add their own twist to the proof. Cicero and Quintilian asserted that a series of questions could provide the necessary information for any given case. This line of questioning is very similar to what you see today in contemporary trials in the court system. They also were enthusiastic about Aristotle's discussion of pathos. Cicero was particularly interested and argued that Pathos should be even more stressed than Aristotle had argued. He felt that appealing to the audience's emotions while progressing solid logic was ideal.

A memorable Cicero quote,

"Six mistakes mankind keeps making century after century: Believing that personal gain is made by crushing others;
Worrying about things that cannot be changed or corrected;
Insisting that a thing is impossible because we cannot accomplish it;
Refusing to set aside trivial preferences;
Neglecting development and refinement of the mind;
Attempting to compel others to believe and live as we do.[15]"

Cicero added to the canon of style by discussing the differences in three types of styles. If you recall, **style** refers to the ways in which something is said, expressed, done, or performed. There are three types of styles: grand, plain, and moderate. Cicero argued that the ideal orator would be able to perform all three types well. The reason for the speech would help the rhetor determine which style was appropriate. The first is the grand style. This is also called *high style.*

The **grand style** is born out of classical rhetoric, or at least that is as far back as we can find evidence of it. The grand style is characterized by heightened emotional attributes that can be seen in the speaker's performance, tone, diction, and figures of speech; it is a writing and speech style that is significant and

---

[13]This webpage reproduces a section of <u>Institutio Oratoria by Quintilian</u> published in Vol. I of the Loeb Classical Library edition, 1920 page 305 http://penelope.uchicago.edu/Thayer/E/Roman/Texts/Quintilian/Institutio_Oratoria/2C*.html#21
[14]This webpage reproduces a section of <u>Institutio Oratoria by Quintilian</u> published in Vol. I of the Loeb Classical Library edition, 1920 page 315 http://penelope.uchicago.edu/Thayer/E/Roman/Texts/Quintilian/Institutio_Oratoria/2C*.html#21
[15]http://www.goodreads.com/author/quotes/13755.Cicero

empowered, impassioned and opulent. Cicero asserted, "the grand orator was fiery, impetuous; his eloquence rushes along with the roar of a mighty stream."

Speakers use a grand style for many reasons, but most come down to four things:

The beauty of the grand style is it has the ability to not merely present information in an interesting way, but also performs the argument in a manner that demands the audience take notice, change their perceptions, and alter their behaviors. Masters of the grand style will consistently have speeches with metaphors, similes, amplifications, the most moving figures of speech, vivid words, and sentences constructed with rhythm in mind. Shakespeare consistently used the grand style in his writing and especially in the monologues of his most impassioned characters. If you choose to use the grand style you will want to choose many different "figures of speech" from the list that is provided.

Although the grand style was the style of choice in classical times, there are two other types of stylistic choices you should be aware of: plain and moderate styles. **Plain style** is also known as *low style* and is characterized as a brief and clear form of speaking. Plain style is not concerned with figurative language, tonal passions, or other things associated with the grand style. The common use of this style is for the delivery of information without the intent to persuade. Speakers who employ this style usually do so for three reasons:

Plain styled speakers will have a lesser chance at influencing the audience's beliefs, attitudes, values, or behaviors. **Moderate style** is the style that incorporates some attributes from both the high and low styles. The goal of moderate style is achieve some emotional impact but also remain simple and clear. Often called the *pleasing style*, moderate style is known for amplification, effective word choice, and vivid language. Aristotle was most fond of this style.

There are many more rhetoricians to mention, but those mentioned in this chapter provide the most foundational information you need in order to move forward. The contributions of the Sophists, Plato, Aristotle, Cicero, and Quintilian are still used in rhetoric to this day. In the pages to come we will introduce you to more contemporary rhetoricians and provide you with a diverse understanding of where rhetoric has been and where it is now.

Here are a few stylistic figures for your consideration:

- **Onomatopoeia**—the use of words that sound like what you are describing.
- **Conduplicatio**—the repetition of words or phrases at the start of successive phrases.
- **Repetition**—the repeating of a word for poetic effect, impact, or draw attention to that idea.
- **Polyptoton**—the repeating of words that come from the same root.
- **Hyperbole**—the use of wild exaggeration for impact or humor.
- **Alliteration**—the repeating of the same sound by words close in proximity. Sometimes alliteration can be as simple as repeating the same consonant letter.
- **Assonance**—the repeating of the same vowel sound.
- **Superlative**—the declaration that something is the best or worst of its kind
- **Epistrophe**—the repetition of the same word or series of words in a sentence, clause, or phrase.
- **Climax**—a figure that builds intensity in the speech by repeating words or phrases while increasing their power or significance.
- **Anagnorisis**—a statement designed to keep your audience from doing something. It is often used in conjunction with hyperbole and cause and effect language strategies.
- **Parallelism**—the use of like structures in two or more different clauses.

Key Terms

Argumentation—The communicative process of advancing, supporting, criticizing, and modifying claims so that appropriate decision makers may grant or deny adherence.

Arrangement—Dictates how a speech or writing should be organized.

Canons of Rhetoric—Invention, arrangement, style, memory, and delivery.

Corax—The man who has the first recorded written rhetoric.

Debate—A method of argumentation, debate is the process of inquiry and advocacy and the seeking of a reasoned judgment on a proposition.

Delivery—Includes verbal utterances and emotional impact but also body language, gestures, and tonal fluctuations.

Dialectic—Allows humans to separate the truth from the false through questioning. Is the pragmatic procedures of argumentation that allow humans to separate the truth from the false through questioning.

Empiricism—Claims humans gain knowledge by experience.

Epistemology—How we come to know; the study of the nature of knowledge.

Ethos—The speaker's credibility.

False Rhetoric—is used by individuals pursuing their own interests rather than arriving at a truth.

Logos—Refers to organization and logic.

Memory—The degree to which an orator remembers her speech and the methods a speaker uses to ensure the audience retains the speech's primary teachings and persuasions.

Pathos—Arguments that are primarily based on appeals to emotions.

Rationalism—Asserts that humans obtain knowledge through reasoning.

Relativism—Knowledge is relative to the limited nature of the mind and the conditions of knowing.

Rhetoric—Is concerned with argumentation as a process. Also widely known as the "art of persuasion."

Sophists—A group of educators who traveled the land city by city offering educational courses to citizens for a price.
Style—The artful expression of ideas.
Tone—Cues to a rhetor's attitude and emotions; the quality of voice.

References

Plato, *Gorgias.* Trans. W.R.M. Lamb. Cambridge, MA: Harvard Univeristy Press, 1967, passim. Print.

Nicholson, Graeme. *Plato's Phaedrus: The Philosophy of Love.* West Lafayette, IN: Purdue University Press, 1999. Print.

James L. Golden, Goodwin F. Berquist, William E. Coleman. *The Rhetoric of Western Thought.* Dubuque, IA: Kendall/Hunt Publishing Co., 1976. Print.

Aristotle. *On Rhetoric: A Theory of Civic Discourse.* Trans. George A. Kennedy. 2nd ed. New York: Oxford University, 2007. Print. 1356b

Thorson, Andrea, Michael Korcock, Mark Staller. *Contemporary Public Speaking: How to Craft and Deliver a Powerful Speech.* Dubuque, IA: Kendall Hunt. eBook.

This webpage reproduces a section of *Institutio Oratoria* by Quintilian published in Vol. I of the Loeb Classical Library edition, 1920 page 305 http://penelope.uchicago.edu/Thayer/E/Roman/Texts/Quintilian/Institutio_Oratoria/2C*.html#21.

Classic figures of speech. http://rhetoric.byu.edu/Figures/S/synonymia.htm

Aristotle. *Rhetoric.* Trans. W. Phys Roberts. New York: The Modern Library, Random House, 1954. Print.

Cicero. *De Oratore.* Trans. E. W. Sutton. Cambridge, MA: Harvard University Press, 1959. Print.

Golden, J, Berquist G, & Coleman W. (2000). *The Rhetoric of Western Thought.* Kendall/Hunt Publishing Company Dubuque, Iowa

Hikins, J. *Remarks on the Development of Rhetoric.* Dubuque, IA: Kendall/Hunt Publishing Company, 1996. Print.

Johnstone, C. Communicating in classical contexts: The centrality of delivery. *Quarterly Journal of Speech* 2001;87(2):121143.

Quintilian. *The Institution Oratoria of Quintilian.* Trans. H. E. Butler. 4 vols. Cambridge: Loeb Classical Library, 1963. Print.

Check Your Understanding

Who were the Sophists and what did they do?

Why did Plato disapprove of the Sophists?

Name and describe the three types of proofs:
1.

2.

3.

What is a quote commonly attributed to Plato?

What is a quote commonly attributed to Aristotle?

What was the relationship between Plato and Aristotle?

Name and describe the five canons of rhetoric
1.

2.

3.

4.

5.

Explain what false rhetoric is and provide a contemporary example of your own.

Summarize Plato's feelings about absolute truth or "transcendent" truth.

Who was Gorgias and what role did he play in teaching rhetoric?

What was Plato's definition of rhetoric and how does it differ from Aristotle's definition of rhetoric?

Aristotle classified discourse into three areas. Define and describe each.

1.

2.

3.

Aristotle articulated four reasons for studying and understanding rhetoric. Name the four here and full explain what you think Aristotle is referring to.

1.

2.

3.

4.

What did Aristotle teach us about pathos? Explore the good and the potential weakness please.

What are three questions we can ask ourselves in an effort to determine our ethos as a speaker?
1.

2.

3.

What is the difference between articulation, enunciation, and pronunciation?

Define and describe the classical arrangement of oration
1.

2.

3.

4.

5.

6.

Who was Cicero and Quintilian and what was their contribution to rhetoric?

Self-Assessment: A brief history of rhetoric to argumentation (unrelated to text)

1. Put these thinkers in chronological order from earliest (1) to latest (6):
   _____ Plato
   _____ Socrates
   _____ Corax
   _____ Aristotle
   _____ The Sophists

2. Match the characteristics to each historical figure:

   _____ Plato   1. Wrote that rhetoric has 3 aspects: pathos, ethos, logos.
   _____ Socrates   2. Excoriated the Sophists, calling them amoral posers .
   _____ Corax   3. The teacher of Plato, a founder of Western Civilization.
   _____ Aristotle   4. Credited by Aristotle as the inventor of rhetoric: the Crow.
   _____ The Sophists   5. Itinerant teachers who taught the arts of persuasion.

3. Give an example of how you have used rhetoric in the last 3 days:

   _____

   _____

   _____

   _____

4. Which of Aristotle's 3 elements of rhetoric are most prominent in each of the following?

   a. The school district needs more money to hire additional teachers to meet our escalating school population. If we don't hire more teachers, class sizes will skyrocket and crowding harms education a lot. The only way to get more money is to vote YES on measure 43.

   b. I have been a medical doctor for over 30 years and have published 43 studies about kidney diseases in the medical journals. I perform over 100 kidney transplants a year. You don't need a kidney transplant.

   c. Think of the kids! The little babies! So adorable, but so vulnerable! We need capital punishment for manufacturers of dangerous toys: stop those murderers!

   d. The Raine study showed that those kids who spoke faster had higher IQ scores. Similarly, the Hulme and Mackenzie results showed that adults who speak faster have better short term memory. Perhaps surprisingly, it appears that speaking faster makes you smarter.

Enunciation Exercises

Stress the sounds while being exaggerative with your face- hyper extend. If you look ridiculous you are doing it correctly.

Stress the "ch," "ed," and "t" sounds

Which witch watched Willy watch Wanda wash windows?

Which wing waived and rocked?

Rest is best when waiting

Walter wagged and wriggled

power-power-power

rye-rye-rye-rye-rye

soothing-soothing-soothing

loathing-loathing-loathing

writhe-writhe-writhe

Sress the "r," ery," "k" and "d" sounds

Reid was eerie, airy, and fiery with fury

Red leather. Yellow leather. Red leather. Yellow leather.

Ryan dreamed of airy brown branches.

Roberta drew drinks of dripping fruit.

My mama made me mash my red m&m's

Stress the "th," "er," and "ing"

Theo thought the weather was soothing

Cathy loathed bathing feathers

Thinking, stinking, pinking

She was thinking and sitting

The mythical thieves thought through the weather

Other favorites

The wolf sat on the roof while the dog wagged the "roofed"

Bitter better butter

Practice With a Peer Worksheet

Practice your arguments/cases with another member of the class. Evaluate some components of delivery. Provide your partner with specific feedback in these areas.

Pitch: _____

_____

Rate: _____

_____

Volume: _____

_____

Enunciation: _____

_____

Pronunciation: _____

_____

Voice quality: _____

Verbal clutter: _____

_____

Posture: _____

Lower body: _____

Upper body: _____

Hand gestures: _____

Facial expressions: _____

Eye contact: _____

3 Contemporary Rhetoric

Chapter Objectives

This chapter will discuss the contributions of rhetoric over the years, starting after the classical era. The contributions to rhetoric have alerted the way we think about and communicate about discourse. The goal of this chapter is to give you a small sampling of diverse contributions to rhetoric since the classical era. Within this chapter, you will learn a variety of perspectives about the nature of rhetoric, the power of rhetoric, and the usefulness of rhetoric.

Contemporary or modern contributions to rhetorical theory are vast and very different. The contributions here are some of the most significant, but there are many more worthy of discussion that we simply do not have time to mention here; those mentioned will be important to your understanding of argumentation and debate for this course and significant to contributions to the discipline. Those mentioned also represent alternative perspectives in an attempt to provide you with a well-rounded understanding of rhetoric. We will end by discussing how ethos and pathos are developed in contemporary rhetoric. Logos, will be discussed in coming chapters in great detail, as such, are not a focus here. In short, in this chapter you will learn:

1. How rhetoric has been used, evaluated, and/or regarded during certain periods in history.
2. How rhetoric can be used as a means of educating, motivating, critiquing, and understanding the world around us in a variety of ways.
3. The ways traditional rhetorical concepts can still be applied and are often applied today.

Rhetoric and Truth

Let us revisit a concept you were introduced to in chapter two. The last chapter began with the discussion of the Sophists and Plato and their disagreement on the nature of truth and the role of rhetoric in obtaining it. When we enter into an argument with someone, we usually try to find the truth, convince others that we know the truth, and persuade them accordingly through dialectic and rhetoric. As such, rhetoric has always had truth at its core. Current uses of rhetoric may mislead you to thinking it is only about style, such as when commentators suggest a politician has "Nothing but empty rhetoric." However, truth is not as simple of a concept as it may appear.

This section of the chapter will focus on the contributions of a variety of rhetoricians over time. There are many different perspectives, influences, and ideas progressed herein. The purpose of this section is not to argue that one rhetorician is right or that one perspective is best, its purpose is to provide you with a variety of ideas to consider while you contemplate the role of rhetoric, the purpose of rhetoric, and what rhetoric actually is. This chapter will not only focus on people who developed theories or principles of rhetoric, but also on those who were skilled rhetoricians, and those who offered original, unique and powerful perspectives on the subject. This is a very small glimpse into some of the rhetoricians over time and is in no way a comprehensive overview of historical rhetorical contributions.

In order to understand what we mean when discussing truth, it is important that you understand where the argument began; we have covered this in the previous chapter. It is also important that we understand a few key conditions of the concept of "truth." The first term is **epistemology**, which is the nature of knowledge or how we come to knowledge. Rhetoricians and philosophers approach epistemology from two standard standpoints: rationalism and empiricism.

Humanism is a philosophy that values the agency and worth of humans. **Empiricism** is the act or method in which humans gain knowledge by experience. **Rationalism** asserts that humans obtain knowledge through reasoning. Rationalists believe there are certain things that are just naturally true, "universally accepted truths," which is sometimes called *a priori* truth. *Priori* is Latin for "first things," or something that must be done first.

You may have heard of "self-evident truths." These truths are written as statements we do not have to think about because they are so obviously "true." Examples of commonly accepted self-evident truths are claims such as: "we exist," or "I cannot be in two places at once." But there are gray areas or areas of disagreement among theorists and philosophers. Another word you should understand is "**postmodernism**," which is a philosophy that analyzes and is critical of the foundational ideas of Western thinking. It is a critical perspective that often focuses on power distribution and effects and the discourse of "truth." The more famous postmodern philosophers were Jean-François Lyotard and Michel Foucault.

Herein you will be presented with diverse rhetorical perspectives. Take note of the ideas that you like and those that you might disagree with. Everything is an argument afterall; there is no truth, only perspective.

Medieval Times and Rhetoric

St. Augustine

Historical contributions regarding rhetoric of the medieval era are marked in religion. Truth became central again as it had in Platonic times. Like Plato, **St. Augustine** believed in ultimate truths, yet St. Augustine believed that truth originated through God, and God sought to speak to humans through the bible. Trained in the art of rhetoric, Augustine began spreading religious "truths" employing his rhetorical knowledge. He wrote about his arriving at truth though the bible in his book *On Christian Doctrine*. This book and much of his teaching was a blend of rhetoric and Christian teaching, thus a form of preaching became an influential conduit of knowledge during the medieval times. His book was intended to teach other religious leaders how to "correctly" interpret the bible and train them to advocate successfully for Christianity.

Christine De Pizan

Christine De Pizan was a pioneering rhetorician of this time. Pizan is most notable for her critique of women's position in society; specifically, she analyzed the stereotypes that persisted in the male-centered arts. Her rhetorical contributions stem from her writing that challenged male writers who incorporated misogynistic beliefs within their literary works, which subsequently trickled down into society. Much of her writing centers on asking women to reclaim their sex and teaches them how to counteract male dominance.

Fundamentally Pizan rhetoric sought to reconstruct the "truth" about her sex. The standards of her time banished woman as inferior objects that were incapable of grasping subjects such as the art of rhetoric, or the goals of dialectics. She created stories that produced counter-narratives to what women were seeing and hearing that the time. Narratives surrounded women largely though the writings of men that placed them in degrading dehumanized stereotypes.

By formulating a female dialogue that celebrated women, she successfully created a new narrative for women; her contributions to rhetoric stem from her persuasive skills in fighting a dominant discourse. Persuasive dialogue was a tool Pizan constructed in an attempt to arrive at truth; a tool provided and created for women that would be felt for centuries to come. She embodied the energy of humanism that provided the power for an individual to know and change the world. She not only provided a means of arriving at truth, but also a means of acting on it. The tenets of humanism asked that individuals understand the art, moral philosophy, and then also the "civic" responsibility.

The Renaissance

Peter Ramus

While the classical era had been a struggle with empiricism and transcendent truths, and the medieval period had been concerned with religious truths, the Renaissance period took a turn and eventually landed on humanism. **Peter Ramus** redefined rhetoric during this time; he transferred invention and arrangement to dialectics. Invention and arrangement were the first two "canons of rhetoric," more simply understood as the first key elements of rhetoric.

Invention was the persuasive core of rhetoric, the stage where the rhetor finds something to say on a given topic. Today we call this brainstorming. If you recall, *arrangement* is the basic organization of a given speech and where a rhetor is strategically placing arguments in order to have the greatest effect. Ramus advocated that arrangement and invention were actually forms of logic and therefore could be replaced with dialectics.

His concept of truth was embedded in his concept of logic. Given that arrangement and invention were now banished canons; memory, style and delivery were left. Fundamentally rhetorical study came to be understood as a way to dress logic and it lost importance and credibility quickly. Given this, arriving at truth through logic no longer emphasized the "artistic" side of rhetoric. Delivery and style fell from the light that Cicero and Quintilian had placed upon them all those years before.

The Enlightenment

Locke and Descartes

The Enlightenment was full of key thinkers regarding rhetoric and truth. **Locke, Hume,** and **Descartes** were large contributors during this time. Enlightenment and epistemology were related on an empirical and rational level. **David Hume** published *A Treatise of Human Nature,* a work that combined empiricism (under Locke's conceptions), which determines the validity of ideas, and thus *the truth.* **René Descartes** focused on the power and importance of deduction. A rationalist, Descartes believed in the "thinking mind," the concept of "I think, therefore I am."

Rationalism vs. Empiricism

Rationalists believe that knowledge is gained outside of experience, mainly through reasoning. Empiricists believe knowledge is gained by experience. Rationalists argue that there are limits to human senses and experience, while empiricists will on occasion, adopt a form of skepticism instead of relying on rationalism, which basically means that when an experience has not been had to prove something then they believe it doesn't exist instead of relying on reasoning to establish a form of understanding.

John Locke and Francis Bacon disagreed. According to Locke and Bacon, **deduction** (which is a formal means of logic—a rational and logical way to come to a "truth") cannot produce truth. Deduction can only convey a way of knowing, which is faulty reasoning. **Induction**, on the other hand, which makes generalizations based on single instances and is often used to generate hypotheses, can produce new knowledge. New knowledge is what science "should" produce. **Rationalism** at this time created the idea that truth can be arrived at through an appeal to reason, which is not exactly negating the tenets of empiricism, but isn't exactly agreeing with them either.

Figure 3.1   John Locke (1632–1704)

Francis Bacon

The Enlightenment was a period in European history that was marked by scientific, political, and philosophical revolutions. As these revolutions altered established notions regarding knowledge and truth, closer attention was paid to the psychological processes of reflection and perception. As a result, rhetoric underwent changes in the way in which it was understood, due largely to the contributions of **Francis Bacon.** Bacon's theory separated the human mind into faculties. Bacon asserted that the human mind has three main faculties which together function as a trinity: memory, imagination, and reason. These faculties allow us to comprehend the "truth." His faculties were greatly studied, and soon rhetoric shifted to appeal to these various faculties of the mind.

Resultant from Bacon's theories was a movement in rhetoric that focused on the power and importance of delivery. This development influenced how rhetoric was studied by shifting the focus towards delivery and away from the other forms. This movement recognized the scientific function of rhetoric (psychology) and psychology's role in persuasion. Because rhetoric became affiliated with scientific processes and scientific reasoning, rhetoric was further recognized as a legitimate area of study.

Bacon made many contributions to rhetoric, but his discussion on the mind always stand apart. Concerned with psychology of the human mind, Bacon was able to argue that humans are susceptible to prejudice and ignorance. He asserts that there are four specific fallacies that should be avoided: "idols of the tribe," "idols of the cave," "idols of the market place," and "idols of the theatre." He

Figure 3.2   Francis Bacon's faculty of the minds: memory, imagination, and reason.

argued that these idols are obstacles to scientific knowledge and analysis. These idols are basically errors due to natural tendencies or prejudices that hinder the mind's ability to accurately understand. Bacon asserts that if we can identify and deal with these idols only then we cannotice and thus refute invalid arguments. His ultimate goal is to remove the clouds of misunderstanding and allow humans to see a clearer, more accurate reflection of reality and logic.

"Idols are false notions which are now in possession of the human understanding, and have taken deep root therein, not only so beset men's minds that truth can hardly find entrance, but even after entrance is obtained, they will again in the very instauration of the sciences meet and trouble us, unless men being forewarned of the danger fortify themselves as far as may be against their assaults."

Idols of the tribe Human nature—humans see the world through a distorted lens. Wishful thinking, our senses, and judgmental nature are the primary problems.

Idols of the cave Education—reliance on one school of thought, customs, tradition, worship of certain authorities, religion or even just personalities—these are things that humans believe in regardless of the lack of evidence that supports the ideas.

Idols of the market place Communication—these errors originated in public communication about ideas or words. Bacon asserts that words that are vague, overly complex, or jargon-based communication hinder clear thinking.

Idols of the theatre Law—dogmatic laws that are followed because that is how it is, versus that is how it was tested and observed would be best. Bacon specifically criticized superstitious thoughts and sophistical and empirical philosophies because they rely on speculation or limited research and evidence.

Mary Astell

Mary Astell is best known for invading the masculine stronghold of traditional rhetoric. Yet still conservative, she developed a theory of rhetoric that is liberating for oppressed groups. She argued for a "separate but equal" model (for example, women's rhetoric should focus on the art of conversation, which is different, but not inferior, to men's focus on the public sphere). Astell asserted that a woman's rhetoric should focus primarily on accommodating her audience. Her great contribution to rhetoric is that she challenged the win/lose tradition of rhetoric. Astell felt there was no need for discussions to be reduced to a mere winner or loser and argued for a nondisputatious model of communication.

She served as a valuable role model for other women and was known for her great skill as an eloquent speaker, argument constructor, and philosopher. Unlike many elitist philosophers before her, Astell wanted her writings to be accessible to the masses. Her rhetoric often

Figure 3.3 Astell believed argumentation did not always have to be about winning or loosing. Her rhetoric focused on balance and equality.

centered on style, clarity, and truth. She believed that humans are naturally attracted to the truth; therefore stylistic ornaments are unnecessary. If you think back to the canons of rhetoric, you can see she valued invention and arrangement more than style and delivery. When she discusses style it is mostly a discussion in clarity to arrive at truth versus ways to employ stylish ways of speaking.

Astell claimed that even the best teachers of eloquence could help only a small amount. It is natural ability that is most important. This was an interesting perspective, if you think back to Quintilian and Cicero who felt style and delivery were extremely important and dedicated their lives to teaching others the skill. Astell's perspective is nearly opposite to theirs. If you recall, Quintilian was actually a very poor speaker and before he was an educator he had given up on civic oratory because he could not gain the skill of projecting his voice, so perhaps Astell's perspective is a valid one. Are delivery and style teachable or inherent?

One of the most important distinguishing features of her rhetoric was her *principle of caring*. **The principle of caring** established that audience members must believe that speakers have their own best interest at heart. She contends that a speaker must have tenderness towards the audience and spare them any humiliations regardless of their absurdity or misguidedness. Her goal was not to win or to triumph over the audience, but rather, to get them to see the truth for their own good. This idea may remind you of the ethos that Aristotle discussed. Ethos concerns the character, good will, and credibility in general. However, Aristotle never fully developed the concept of caring.

19th Century

Langer, Bain, Hill, Whately, and Coleridge

Arguably, the most notable historical development that influenced how rhetoric was studied during the 19th century was the **breaking off of rhetoric from composition**. In the mid 19th century, written composition had become imbedded in rhetoric as one field. There was immense pressure during this period for one to be accomplished in the skill of writing effectively. Eventually, rhetoric was slowly detached from composition as composition became more about efficiency. **Alexander Bain, Adams Hill, Richard Whately,** and **S. T. Coleridge** are given some credit for the eventual parting of rhetoric from composition. The breaking off of rhetoric from composition serves as a significant historical development because it marks the moment when rhetoric was given the opportunity to be taught without the overture of composition or what you would understand today as the discipline of English. It marked the time when the role of rhetoric in academia was redefined, reborn, and for the first time, was studied as its own discipline. This break-up forever changed the way rhetoric was taught, considered, and studied.

Susanne K. Langer was able to postulate an incredibly significant contribution to rhetoric regarding symbolism and meaning. Langer argued that the foundation to human understanding and epistemology (ways of knowing) lies in symbolism. Langer was among the first to discuss how symbols construct our reality and that language creates symbols and our language is affected by our cultures. Langer's work, *Philosophy in a New Key*, discussed how language structures our perception. In a presentation on the famous rhetor, Arabella Lyon (1988) states,

> *"What Langer did, so essential to the rebirth of rhetoric, was to represent meaning as both socially constructed and achieved collaboratively by rhetor and audience. Breaking with earlier tradition and prevailing thought in the 1940s by refocusing three key concerns with language, Langer (1) suggested the purpose of symbolization is not just*

communication, nor primarily communication, but rather a unique human need to express individual conceptions of the world, to create form, and, so, a reality; (2) broadened the understanding of what reason is by connecting all human thought to feeling, that is, the "sensuous experience" of the world; and (3) portrayed an interactive relationship of mutual interpretation between the rhetor and audience whose thoughts and language are pinioned by society."

Other Contributions

Friedrich Nietzsche

Understanding how truth is a reflection of perspective rather than a discovery of an absolute certainty is essential to understanding Nietzsche's contributions to rhetorical theory. Nietzsche's views on perspectivism reduce epistemology to psychology in many ways (yet I use the word *reduce* lightly). The rise of morality and of moral disputes thus becomes a matter of psychology.

Nietzsche has contributed a montage of remarks about truth in his works, yet he was not so much concerned with the best way to arrive at truth or the origination of truth as were Plato and others of the past. Nietzsche was more concerned with the effects "truths" have on a given audience. He indicates how claims of truth coerce agreement and conformity and blind real truths. Unlike many before him, he does not attempt nor claim to have come up with some universal truth or a method of truth; rather he is interested in how conceptions of truth function in a society and how they affect a given society. He is interested in questions of ontology (the nature of being) and epistemology (the nature of knowledge); as such, his thoughts are more social and psychological than philosophical. He seeks to free humans from their "false consciousness" and attempts to change society's dominate structures.

Figure 3.4   Friedrich Nietzsche.

Whereas Aristotle sought to concentrate on the audience, Nietzsche concentrates on human agency. His focus is on the individual and the human will. The idea of empiricism is not present here, nor is necessarily humanism, relativism, or positivism; his ideas transcend nearly all these categories. His work is important to rhetoric because he expanded what is considered rhetoric, and thus rhetorical artifacts, by claiming all language is rhetorical. Because humans are biased and prejudiced, they are tainted by experience and assumption, by culture and expectation. One's conception of truth depends on the perspective from which one speaks. Truth thus depends on a person's perspective.

Given this, Nietzsche's primary argument is that there is no truth outside of a person's own individual perspective. A transcendent truth as Plato discussed is not possible in Nietzsche's worldview. Nietzsche's opinion here has caused unrest in many rhetoricians and philosophers because, if Nietzsche is correct, how can any of us make any valid claims or theories that are valid to anyone other than ourselves?

In *Beyond Good and Evil*, Nietzsche argues that there is a lack of integrity on the part of philosophers who present their ideas as an *ultimate truth* and a product of pure reason. He states, "they pose as having discovered and attained their real opinions through the self-evolution of a cold, pure, divinely unperturbed dialectic: while what happens at bottom is that a *prejudice*, a notion, an 'inspiration,' generally a desire of the heart sifted and made abstract, is defended by them with reasons sought after the event."

Nietzsche asserts that often we have many illusions of truth; we forget that we created these illusions, and then we accept them as truths. Because we place our subjective opinions on issues and ideas and put those opinions into our own words or language, we negotiate meanings of ideas and arrive at a socially constructed and acceptable form of truth but not necessarily the "absolute truth." Truth is fundamentally a construction of a given language. Nietzsche is arguing that, because humans created words that represent various objects and ideas, we are in a sense constructing a truth.

We can ask, what are the illusions that pass as truths in science and by what rhetoric do we come to believe them? Basically everything becomes rhetoric according to Nietzsche's argument, because we must consider the person who is arriving at the "logical conclusion" or "truth" as a way of understanding that truth. Perception and prejudice plague philosophers' works because of their own experiences and subjective interpretations and word choice. For the most part, Nietzsche believes the audience is unaware of the biases and prejudices of the authors and asks that we begin to consider the perspective of authors when considering their claims of truth.

Unlike Plato, Nietzsche is not a believer in humans' ability to arrive at an absolute truth. Nietzsche contends "I shall reiterate a hundred times that 'immediate certainty,' like 'absolute knowledge' and 'thing in itself,' contains a *contradictio in adjecto* [contradiction in terms]: we really ought to get free from the seduction of words!" This does not mean he doesn't believe that there are absolute truths out there, but rather he is skeptical of human's ability to obtain them. He does believe there are degrees of truthfulness and one can get close to truth but never be absolutely certain that their derived truth is the *ultimate truth*, largely because our understanding of what is true is our culture's understanding and our perspectives always influence what is seen as good.

Mikhail Bakhtin

Mikhail Bakhtin centers his understanding of rhetoric in culture. He argues that all discourse is ideological because language is subjective—words are able to construct a truth, a world, a perspective, etc. This means then that spoken or written work is never capable of being unbiased and neutral; it is saturated in the values of the speaker, the listeners, the readers, and it is constructed by the symbols used (words). Fundamentally, Bakhtin argues that when we create discourse we engage in self-disclosure because all language written and spoken has our system of beliefs and values attached to it and these are all influenced by cultures. The second reason he believes rhetoric is ideological is because words have two meanings—the meaning the speaker intends and the meaning the audience perceives. This means that the meaning of any given word or rhetorical act depends on the interpretation of at least two people—the speaker and the audience.

Kenneth Burke

Kenneth Burke and **Lloyd Bitzer** are arguable the two most famous rhetoricians who argue a **contextual and situational theory of rhetoric**. This perspective asserts that "a piece of discourse must be judged against the cultural and situational contexts in which it was produced and in which it is being interpreted" (as qtd in. Herrick, 2005, p. 222). Burke believed that the greatest problem is that humans have separation and alienation. He believed rhetoric was the key to bringing people back together. Burke argued that because humans find so many differences they disassociate and separate; rhetoric has the power to demonstrate similarities and create identification. Of the concept of identification he writes that identification is an antidote or necessary remedy for our alienation from one another.

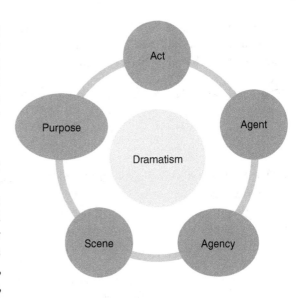

According to Burke, rhetoric alone had the power to bring humans together, and this was accomplished by the use of unifying symbols, common meaning, and ways of acting together that inspired cooperation—not separation. In sum, Burke's primary goal was to use the power of rhetoric to bring humans towards peace, to lesson divides, such as prejudices, cultural misunderstandings, and positions in society, and ultimately lead us to a peaceful existence. Burke also contributed to rhetorical analysis, with his **dramatism technique**. This technique is often referred to as pentadic analysis. This rhetorical analysis is a way of looking at any given rhetorical act to understand the motive: act, scene, agent, agency, and purpose. Burke argued that life was fundamentally one big drama and, if we wanted to discover the motives of people, we could simply examine the motives in their actions and discourse. According to Burke, a character (person) will stress one of those areas over the other and that will tell you their motives.

Robert Solomon

Robert Solomon (1996) explains, "Perspectives and interpretations are always subject to measure, not by comparison with some external 'truth,' perhaps, but by evaluation in their context and according to the purposes for which they are adopted" (p. 196). His perspective is an interpretation and extension of Nietzsche's thoughts on truth. It is essential to Nietzsche that humans understand that the truths they arrive at are affected by society and their own perspectives, but he also recognizes that humans need to act as though the truths they come to are real truths in order to have a good life. He contends that humans should not and cannot act as if they are constantly uncertain of their opinions. Therefore, a person must commit to her actions as a true and just thing.

In sum, he wants us to recognize that our conception of truth is always influenced by our own perspectives and cultures, that an ultimate truth is not obtainable because of this, and yet, it is important that we get as close to our truth as possible and act in its inspiration. An extreme simplification of this idea could be understood in the following example. Ask yourself what you are reading right now. Is it a book? or A packet? Let's say you choose that it is a book. Why did you come to that truth? Why are you so certain it is a book? Could it be a bird? or A table? Fundamentally, you believe this is a book because from the time you were young you were told that such things are books. You were told that items with paper, with bindings, and holding information in typed form that is written by authors on a given subject are books. You have accepted this as a truth.

Nietzsche would say that it is not an ultimate truth that this is a book. He would contend that we have accepted that "truth," but it is not an *absolute truth*. Accepting that truth allows us to function more easily in our surroundings. We must act as if we fully believe this thing you are reading is a *book* or chaos will ensue and we will be in an endless argument. So, it is a book. But that is not an "ultimate truth" rather just "a truth," which has been shaped largely by our surroundings and perspectives.

*****Deconstruction** is a method of analysis that is critical in nature and breaks something down into small parts.

Bell Hooks

bell hooks's major contributions to rhetoric are in her analysis of language distortion and issues of class. Her writings focus on issues of race, glass, sex, gender, and apparatuses of oppression. The role of language in the acquisition of oppression and the dissemination of prejudice is at the core of hooks arguments. Most of her works, well over 50 books and articles, are considered postmodern. hooks purposely lowercases her name as a means of communicating to her audience that her ideas, analysis, and arguments are the most important.

Beginning with Corax, we can see how language and those with access to education of how to become skilled orators was a tool for great power. Hooks argues that today it is no different. She points out that today we still have issues of accessible education and therefore this lack of fair access results in oppression and elitism, and prejudices. The language of liberation has been distorted to reinforce and secure the privileged class. The Sophists were the first to make rhetoric and the skills of language accessible to the masses, but even the Sophists asked for money, and therefore that education was still not accessible to the lower and lowest classes. Hooks asserts that theories are reserved for the elite, based on the language.

Her goal it seems is to unite feminist theory with practical application to people's lives. This kind of dedication is similar to the teachers like Quintilian and even the Sophists. She is also similar to Bacon in the sense that he too believed humans were tainted by bias and prejudice. Bacon also asserted that words can be used to hinder the ability for some to understand. HooksI think would agree, as she asserts that some of the jargon or terminology that is used by the dominate culture is not as understood by other cultures. We may all speak English, for instance, but we still have very different languages—words have different meanings.

Hooks brought the discourse of feminist theory out of the complex, elite level it had gone to, which denied women outside of the academy an understanding of it, and she dedicated herself to reconciling these two camps. She argued that, in order for education to be liberating, we must create theory that is meaningful and can be contextualized within the lived experiences of all students. A primary concept hooks discusses in her books is the idea of the self-reflective and vulnerable educator, which is the simple act of "sharing" one's experiences. Shared experiences are a powerful way to connect and create shared meaning and, yet, this form of educating is often discouraged in contemporary society.

Hooks writes, "ideally, education should be a place where the need for diverse teaching methods and styles would be valued, encouraged, seen as essential to learning." Her primary goal is to create strategies to achieve critical awareness and engagement. hooks's concept of invention is different than the classical rhetoricians' in that it requires the rhetor to invent "alternative habits," to transform the way people think about and perform oppression. It almost seems as if hooks is echoing Quintilian with this by saying that rhetoric should only work for good—in this case, good being the work for human rights." All struggles must be acknowledged simultaneously in order to make any real changes. And change is at the core of her rhetoric. More than anything, she aims to inspire others to use rhetoric for good and to recognize how language can reinforce dominations and oppressions and to act to reduce this.

As you can see, the contributions to rhetoric have been immense since the times of Aristotle and Plato and Cicero and Quintilian. Over the years rhetoricians have perfected and enhanced the canons of rhetoric, they have considered the concept of audience more deeply, they have analyzed and created methods of critiquing language and discourse, and they have dissected the ways discourse serves to construct and maintain oppression and power structures in society. This chapter was a small glimpse into the deep and beautiful sea of rhetorical theory and criticism. For a more concentrated study of these contemporary rhetors, theorists, or critics we recommend reading their original works.

Sonya K. Foss

"Human experiences that are spatially oriented, nonlinear, multidimensional, and dynamic often can be communicated only through visual imagery or other nondiscursive symbols. To understand and articulate such experiences require attention to these kinds of symbols" (143)

Foss, Sonja K. "Framing the Study of Visual Rhetoric."

Sonya K Foss is a Communication Professor in the U.S.A. Her areas of expertise include, but are not limited to rhetorical theory and criticism, feminist perspectives on communication, and visual rhetoric. Foss has contributed mountains of work to the communication discipline and is applauded for her decisive and fresh philosophies. One of her more compelling contributions is in the area of visual rhetoric.

Visual rhetoric is equally as powerful as verbal rhetoric and in some cases more so. Traditional rhetoric only considered the spoken persuasion, but there is an entire world of visual rhetoric out there. We are bombarded with images everyday, each of them trying to convince us to do something, to think something, or to question. Advertisements, the way we dress and wear our hair, television, film, buildings, beers, sodas, and jewelry; all these things speak to us and have significant contemporary implications and meanings. Visual rhetoric is conceptualized as a communicative artifact when rhetors use visual symbols to create communication. By definition visual rhetoric is an artifact that this two or three dimensional, thus paintings, architecture, drawings, and furniture will all classify as visual rhetoric.

Foss and other visual rhetor's assert that there are three markers of visual rhetoric: 1) the image must be symbolic, 2) involve human intervention, 3) and be presented purposefully to an audience. As visual rhetoric examines visual imagery as a communicative artifact, it has the potential to be analyzed as rhetoric. Visual rhetorical analysis examines, three specific components of visual images: 1) their nature, their function, and their evaluation.

Foss proposed a useful way to evaluate visual imagery from a rhetorical perspective. She called it a schema. The schema comes in three parts:

1. The function(s) communicated by the image
2. Assessment of the degree to which substantive and stylistic dimensions of the image support the communication of the function
3. Evaluation of the legitimacy of the function

The easiest way to understand this form of rhetorical analysis is to show you. Take a look at the visual rhetoric (advertisement) from the web address https://www.facebook.com/pages/WALLE-is-a-PC-and-EVE-is-a-Mac/282187517277.

Now, let's apply Sonya K. Foss's Schema step number one; identify the function communicated. Glancing back at the images you can easily determine that one robot is old, rusty, dented, and dirty, while the other robot is clean, contemporary, appealing, and looks efficient. The image is thus communicating that MACs are clean, contemporary and efficient, while PS's are not, which is evident by the dirty and older version representing the PC.

Next, let's apply the second step; assessment of the degree to which substantive and stylistic dimensions of the image supports the communication of the function. Evaluation of the colors used in the images shows us that the PC has dull colors and colors associated with dirt and damage, while the Mac displays a crisp clean white and vibrant contemporary blue hue. The dings and colors displayed on the PC communicate that if I were to purchase a PC it would likely be less efficient, run slower, not move as easily, be clunky or seen as old. The MAC robot has happy squinting eyes, as if to say "I'm so happy to be a MAC." The "hands" and eyes on the PC robot are in positions that communicate sadness or disappointment.

The third step is to evaluate the legitimacy of the function. This is similar to deductive reasoning. Anyone who has seen the movie knows that one robot is smart, fast, and able to do much more than the older looking Wall-E robot, whose only real talent is collecting and compressing trash; this sends quite a message to the audience. Given the information presented it seems that purchasing a MAC computer would be a better investment and make me look a lot cooler.

© Vladimir Arndt, 2014. Used under license from Shutterstock, Inc.

While this was a cute and light-hearted rhetorical analysis, we can also do this same process on more serious and emotional images that reflect disappointing realities of our world. Visual rhetoric can reflect values and beliefs and argue for their support. Visual rhetorical analysis can permit us a way to see what we don't normally, what we choose to ignore, or understand our cultures better. Visual rhetoric has the ability to make an argument in a unique way and it is very powerful. Sonja K. Foss is one of the leaders in this area and someone who helped define this area of rhetoric. Consider these other images. What are they arguing?

Contemporary Elements of a Classical Foundation

Contemporary Ways to Establish Your Ethos

Now that you understand how the definition of, study of, and philosophies of rhetoric have changed over time, let's discuss two of the three major foundations of rhetoric in contemporary terms; ethos and pathos. As you recall, ethos in classical terms refers to the speaker's character. Ethos is directly linked to the audience's perception of the rhetor having good intentions, good character and ethics. To increase your ethos nowadays we tend to select evidentiary support from sources the audience views as reliable. We also select support that is generalizable and valid. Statistics and quotations are a standard part of most speeches, but if you can

© Ivelin Radkov, 2014. Used under license from Shutterstock, Inc.

Figure 3.5 Contemporary argumentation relies heavily on ethical use of evidence and displays of good will.

pick some from the "right" sources you can significantly strengthen your ethos. When deciding which information is the best for your given audience, assess whether your audience views the source as relevant, trustworthy, respectable, and/or tends to reflect their values, attitudes, and beliefs. For instance, if you are going to give a speech on the current rate of obesity in America and you found statistics from a doctor who is relatively unknown and you also found a statistic from the American Medical Association; you should choose the American Medical Association because it is recognizable, respected, and deemed credible by most. If you were giving a speech about how to store your guns to a group of people who already own guns you might consider using the National Rifle Association (NRA), which is an organization that supports decreasing gun control, promotes firearm use and awareness, and has donated millions to help their ideology in policy. If, however, you were giving that same speech to a room of people who do not own guns, who are against gun ownership, or who support gun control, picking the NRA as a source would only decrease your ethos.

Psychographic Considerations

Psychological characteristics of your audience have become important considerations when arguing. Rhetoricians nowadays frequently examine the attitudes, beliefs, and values of their intended audience in order to craft the most effective argument. Research has shown that educated audiences tend to be more open-minded but they also tend to have highly developed points of view. There are three areas of psychological consideration: attitudes, values, and beliefs.

Attitudes

An audience's attitude on a given issue refers to their tendency to think about that topic in a generally negative or positive way. For instance, if you felt Pop Tarts® were better than Toaster Strudel®, this would be an attitude you hold. Attitudes are psychological predispositions to feel a certain way about something.

Values

The tendency to feel that something is right or wrong is a reflection of values. Values indicate an audience's perception of right and wrong. It does not reflect attitude or preference; it merely asserts a level of importance and desirability regarding a set of principles. For instance, you may value your personal rights, freedom, or independence.

Beliefs

Systems of beliefs are a set of accepted truths. A person comes to a belief based on interpretation and judgment. Beliefs are different than values because it is not concerned with right or wrong—beliefs are often "faith" based. An example of belief is a person's choice of religion or belief that humans have a responsibility to be forgiving and kind.

Knowing your audience's attitude, beliefs, and values about your topic beforehand is helpful because it can help you craft your overall message. If you can manage to have guessed

Figure 3.6 Religion is a system of beliefs. It is not a provable truth or an arguable value.

the correct psychological and demographical characteristics, you can include appeals that influence your audience more directly. You can use evaluative appeals that motivate different segments of your audience to agree, become interested, or merely openly listen to your message.

Language and Meaning

You must select your language carefully and consider the way in which different members of an audience may interpret what you say. No one group, culture, or person is right or wrong in their conception of a word, we are each able to have our associations, but when you are a public speaker you have an obligation to choose language that resonates with your audience, is appropriate, and that your audience will understand.

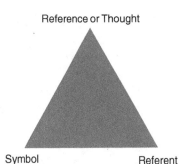

Figure 3.7   The Semantic Triangle of Meaning.

In 1923, Ogden and Richards created a model to communicate these same ideas; The Semantic Triangle of Meaning. The Semantic Triangle of Meaning helps demonstrate how language choices can be understood. The triangle begins in the lower left corner with symbol. In this case, symbol refers to the specific term, word, or phrase that a speaker uses. The next part of the triangle is the lower right referent. Referent refers to the denotative meaning of the word—what the symbol (word) represents. The final area is the reference or thought. Reference refers to the connotative meaning of the word or phrase and/or its historical representation. The reference can hold emotional and physiological responses as well.

Let's say we use the phrase "an act of terror." In America before September 11, the phrase, "an act of terror" didn't hold much value to us beyond the denotative meaning. Now, after September 11, when Americans hear the phrase, "an act of terror," there is a great emotional and physiological response by many Americans. Some people will have a flashback to that day, others will feel anger and fear, and still other people will equate that phrase to a particular group of people. The triangle demonstrates how although we may all understand the denotative meaning of the word we may not have the same connotative understandings.

For example, we may have different emotional and thought-based reactions to hearing the terms based on our own personal and historical connections to a word or phrase. Consider using the semantic triangle when you encounter a term you are questioning using. Try to determine what possible reference the audience may have for that term before using it blindly.

The history of language is built in categories and ways of thinking. Language is fundamentally a learned and accepted process. There are **denotative** and **connotative** meanings to language; each of these types adds a dimension of power to a word. Denotative meaning reflects the dictionary definition of the term or concept. Connotative meaning reflects the attached meaning and commonly associated emotional intent of the word. For instance, the denotative meaning of childish is "childlike." The connotative meaning can be anything from immature, selfish, etc. If you are trying to communicate that someone isimmature or selfish,then childish isa good language choice. If, however, you were trying to point out someone is free, young at heart, and happy, the term "youthful" would be better because it has less negativeconnotations. From person-to-person or culture-to-culture there are various degrees of and understandings for connotation. For instance, consider the popular phrase "hot mess." In recent years the younger generations have taken on that phrase and used it to evaluate people.

Establishing a Similarity

Establishing a sense of similarity with your audience will add to the perceived level of ethos they assign to you. If the audience can identify with you they are more likely to believe you are a credible speaker. One way to increase the audience's identification with you is to use language familiar to them. For instance, if you are speaking to a group of military personnel you should employ language like "fourteen hundred hours" instead the more casual and commonly used "2 p.m." because, although that language may be less familiar to you, it is familiar to them. If you used the "2 p.m." choice you would create a dissimilar climate and lessen your chances to build ethos. Tip: Using Humor. When it is appropriate for the topic and occasion, use a joke or some humor to lighten the mood and create a sense of likability

Use a shared experience to bond with your audience. Choosing stories to illuminate your topic is always a nice choice, but it can also serve to heighten your ethos if you pick a story with which the audience can identify. If there is a time when you can discuss an event you and your audience were both privy to earlier, it could serve as a shared experience that therefore boosts your ethos. The audience tends to feel a connection with speakers who have had similar life experiences and/or similar situational experiences. So, play up the similarity in experience and watch your audience's level of trust soar.

Using sources, statistics, and visual aids that resonate with your audience will also increase your ethos. When you are creating your speech, you have the ability to pick any number of stories, visual aids and/or examples to bring your arguments to life. Try picking the ones that the audience will relate to and the ones that will create the biggest impact. When it comes to statistics, try to use sources that are recognizable and respected, the kinds of names everyone knows to be reliable and respected. For instance, if you are using a news source, picking the *New York Times* over the *Orlando Daily* is a good idea. The *New York Times* is easily recognized and has a reputation of good reporting, whereas the other source lacks recognition and automatic credibility. Always evaluate your sources and visual aids for their level of trustworthiness, similarity to your audience, authority, and reputation.

Be knowledgeable on your topic. This is perhaps the most important tip overall. The more prepared you are, the more confident, at ease, and reliable you seem. If your audience believes you have spent a substantial amount of time researching and understanding your topic fully they will respect you more and view you as an expert, which increases your ethos. Remember that ethos is about perception, so even if you do a lot of research and have become an expert in your area, you also need to be perceived as an expert which means your delivery of the information should be performed in a polished, well-practiced, confident, and meaningful way.

Telling stories is important to your audience believing you mean what you say. Telling stories can lead your audience to trust you more, believe you are like them, and even be more likely to be affected by

To Increase Your Ethos

- Use audience-acceptable sources
- Consider psychographics
- Consider your language
- Establish a sense of similarity
- Use sources, statistics, and visual aids that resonate
- Be knowledgeable
- Use shared experiences
- Tell stories
- to prove your commitment

your appeals to emotion (just be sure you embed stories in logic and reasoning, don't allow stories to be your only evidence). Take, for example, a speech on leukemia. I could provide my audience with a true account of a child who has overcome and smiled through all the pain. This could be effective and make the audience feel some empathy for the child. But, if I instead told the audience I visited this boy twice a week for two semesters and told them stories about how we finger-painted together and how I would always pinch his nose "for luck" before I left, the audience would be much more likely be empathetic, to trust my recommendation, to donate time, to fundamentally have a change in their attitudes, behaviors, and beliefs. Working on improving these areas of ethos does not guarantee the audience will accept your position; however, it does provide them with more reasons to believe you, which should provide you with ample opportunity to present your ideas.

Contemporary Ways to Increase Your Pathos

So what can we do to make our speeches emotionally appealing? Using meaningful language, emotional tone, emotion-evoking examples, stories of emotional events, and general delivery can advance pathos. The first rule in pathos is to be yourself! Pathos should not be manipulative and it is not about putting on a show. If your audience suspects you are doing this, your ethos will be negatively affected.

Pathos should first begin from the heart. Be honest and authentic. The appeal to the audience emotions needs to begin with your own emotional connection. Pathos should be you sharing your emotion with others and thereby evoking an emotional response from them. If you share your passion with them in an honest, organic and meaningful way they will respect you and be more likely to be persuaded by your message.

Narratives

When trying to appeal to emotions, be sure to include emotion-evoking examples, stories, and events. Stories are often the fastest and surest way to make a meaningful connection with your audience. They have also been deemed the most memorable parts of a speech. There is always a restriction on the time you have to give your speech, be sure that there is at least one main point or sub-point that has the potential to be infused with an attempt to gain audience empathy or inspire emotional reaction by way of example or narrative.

For instance, if you were arguing a position that Americans should donate blood, you could include a story that enhances the statistics and logic you present. You might insert a true story about a young girl or boy in your local community who is alive today because of the blood that people donated. Giving people a real human in their own community permits them to see this act as more than just an act, but as an effort to save the life of a person they may actually know. Tip: Do not go too far with your examples. If the audience feels like you are using an extreme example or a story that is embellished you will hurt your ethos.

Meaningful Language Choices and Delivery

There are four components to speaking with meaningful language

1. This means the audience should feel as though you mean what you say. You should display acts of passion in your word choice. A speaker who clearly deeply cares what they are saying will be more likely to motivate, inspire, and persuade their audience. Keep in mind a helpful question that will inspire you to show your passion: If the audience doesn't think you passionately care about this topic, why should they?

2. **Avoid manipulation.** Public address should always have the best interest of the listeners at heart. It is not about putting on a show. If your audience suspects you are doing this, your ethos will be negatively affected. Do not speak unethically. In public speaking the speech to persuade must benefit the audience, not just the speaker's interests.

3. **Be honest and authentic.** The appeal to the audience's emotions needs to begin with your own emotional connection. Pathos should be you sharing your emotion with others and thereby evoking an emotional response from them. If your audience feels you are being honest, and true to yourself, they are more likely to be affected by emotional appeals. **Note different forms of debate call for different levels of pathos***

4. **Use emotion-evoking words.** Words can be emotionally charged or emotionally neutral. In a speech you want to have both, but it is important you have emotionally charged words when you are trying to affect the audience's emotional state. An easy reference to this type of emotional wording is found in everyday politics. Depending on the side and depending on the motive, political parties will describe the same events very differently and usually for the purpose of inspiring an emotional reaction from its listeners.

In recent years, the term "terrorist" has been used frequently by politicians and news anchors; and for a very specific reason. The term "terrorist" has been shown to inspire emotions of anger, pride, and a sense of justice, revenge, and protection. Consider, if those speeches used the term "fighter," or "fanatic" instead of "terrorist"? This is exactly why politicians and the media use the word so much, it gets more attention. It doesn't have the same effect does it? Of course, keep ethics in mind when choosing your emotionally charged terms; we never want to blur the line into lying.

Vivid and sensory words are types of emotionally charged words. These terms evoke very specific emotional responses in listeners that they feel are connected to those terms. For example if you asked the audience to recall the first time they touched the "soft, fresh, dewy, skin of a newborn baby," you would be using vivid sensory words. Vivid sensory words are near opposites of vague and abstract words. Consider the following:

1. We experienced rainy weather.
2. The sharp wet snow pierced my bare skin in the midst of thick and angry pour.

Which of those examples evoked an emotional response or made you see what you were reading? In this example it becomes clear which was the more powerful and captivating sentence. Now, to be clear, it is not good to constantly use these kinds of words, but if you want to affect your audience and affect their emotions your speech must employ some of these word choices and you must deliver them confidently and with ethos.

Proximity

You may also increase your pathos in a speech by getting closer to your audience. Moving physically closer to your audience is one way to establish a connection and make yourself more personable (please respect personal space of course). If you have a podium in front of you, move it to the side or step around it and come in front of it so the audience can see you better and so that you can walk to different places in the room to establish better eye contact and a sense of immediacy. When the room is not full, ask that the audience move to the seats closest to you. It has been widely established that the closure you are to your audience, the more personal your presentation feels for them. The closer the audience feels to you the greater impact your emotional appeals will have.

To Increase Your Pathos

1. Be yourself
2. Use emotionally charged words ethically
3. Use vivid and sensory words
4. Use tonal variation to impact the audience more
5. Use emotion-evoking examples & stories
6. Get closer to your audience

Make Your Language Clear and Simple[1]

1. *Use familiar words.* Using words your audience is unfamiliar with will result in them feeling isolated or thinking about the word instead of what you are actually trying to say. Unfamiliar words are distracting.
2. *Make sure your sentences can be easily understood.* When you write a complex sentence you have the ability to choose from comas, semicolons, colons, periods, etc. And all these options allow your sentence to read in a certain way. In speech making we have no such tools, so we need to make sure our delivery is impeccable (see the delivery chapter) and that we are communicating in a way that is easily understood.
3. *Use concrete instead of vague words.* Concrete words are simple, to the point, and they tend to have less chance of connotation issues. **Concrete** language references a specific object. **Vague** language (often termed abstract) is ambiguous language that is less clear in what it is references. In public speaking it is generally expected that you use more concrete terms to avoid misunderstandings or unintended interpretations[2].

Contemporary Delivery Exercises

As expressed earlier, enunciation and articulation are fundamental to your credibility as a speaker. Given this, it is important that you become skilled at enunciation and articulate thoughts and ideas in a clear manner. Below you will find the most common sounds with which speakers struggle. These exercises will help you become a more articulate speaker. Depending on where you are from, you likely forget to pronounce some consonants in words or you tend to slur the ends of your words. These exercises will help you get crisp clear diction and leave those nasty inarticulate habits behind you.

You need to start out very slowly and deliberately, enunciating and pronouncing each sound over and over until you do it correctly three times in a row. Once you master it, quicken the pace but maintain accuracy. Until you are an exceptionally skilled speaker, the rule to know is, if you think you are over enunciating, you are doing it just right. When you feel like you are doing it just right or enough, you are not doing it good enough.

Once you have mastered the single words then progress to the sentences. Say the sentences over and over and at faster and faster speeds. Once you have a fast rate down, try to emphasize various words within the sentence and say each sentence with various emotions. For instance, say the sentence with excitement and emphasize the third andfifth words. Then say the sentence with other emotions, such as anger, sadness,

---

[1]Thorson et. al 2013 Contemporary Public Speaking Kendall Hunt –
[2]Thorson et. al 2013.

confusion, irritation, and surprise, and choose different words to emphasis with a tonal change. For best results practice a minimum of three minutes three times a day. I recommend doing them in the moments you already have free, like car rides, showers, or while getting dressed.

Contemporary Enunciation Exercises

Which witch watched Willy watch Wanda wash windows?
Which wing waived and rocked?

Stress the "r," "ery," "k," and "d" sounds
Reid was eerie, airy, and fiery with fury.
Red leather. Yellow leather. Red leather. Yellow leather.
Ryan dreamed of airy brown branches.
Roberta drew drinks of dripping fruit.
My mama made me mash my red M&M's.

Stress the "th," "er," and "ing"
Theo thought the weather was soothing.
Cathy loathed bathing feathers.
Thinking, stinking, pinking
She was thinking and sitting.
The mythical thieves thought through the weather.

Other favorites
The wolf sat on the roof while the dog wagged the "roofed."
Bitter better butter
My dad made bitter butter better than my butler.
Keep crashing and smashing while bashing and mashing.
Watching walking rotting stalking
Toy boat toy boat toy boat
Which toy boat rocked?

Other verbal elements that contribute to a successful appeal to pathos include:

1. Pitch: How high or low your voice is
2. Rate: How fast or slow you speak
3. Volume: How loudly or softly you speak
4. Enunciation: How clearly you say your words
5. Pronunciation: How correctly you say your words
6. Accent or dialect: Regional variations in how words are pronounced
7. Voice quality: The particular quality of your voice, such as "raspy" or "nasal"
8. Verbal clutter: Filler words that clutter your verbal communication

---

[3]Thorson, Staller, Korcok, 2014 Contemporary Public Speaking: How to Craft and Deliver a Powerful Speech. Kendall Hunt Publishing

Additionally, there are at least eight visual elements to be aware of when standing before a public speaking audience.

1. Use of space: Where you position your body in relation to the audience
2. Posture: How you hold your body when you are sitting or standing
3. Lower body movement: The movement of your hips, legs, and feet
4. Upper body movement: The movement of your head, shoulders, and torso
5. Hand gestures: Hand movements used to reinforce your verbal messages[3]
6. Facial expressions: Combinations of facial features used to convey emotions
7. Eye contact: Direct gaze between the speaker and audience members
8. Personal appearance: Appearance of the speaker created by grooming and clothing

Conclusion

Moving forward you will learn about logos, the foundation of rhetoric that focuses on reasoning. The next two sections will be devoted to dissecting the various kinds of appeals to logos possible in the realm of debate and argumentation. Given what you have learned about the history of rhetoric, and the ways in which ethos and pathos are established try to find a balance in your argumentation. As you move to the final section of this text, donot forget this first section. Remember the foundation, remember the cannons, the power of ethos and pathos, and even less traditional forms and roles of rhetoric that may prove useful.

References

Laval, V., A. Bert-Erboul. (2005). French-speaking children's understanding of sarcasm: The role of intonation and context. *Journal of Speech, Language & Hearing Research*, 48(3): 610 620.

Sansavini, A., J. Bertoncini, G. Giovanelli. (1997). Newborns discriminate the rhythm of multisyllabic stressed words. *Developmental Psychology* 33, 3–11.

Bolton, J. 2003 The garnishing of the manner of utterance. Western States Communication Association.

Botinis, A., M.B. Granstro, B. Mobius. (2001). Developments and paradigms in intonation research. *Speech Communication*. 33: 263–296.

Campbell, K. (1997). *Critiques of Contemporary Rhetoric*. Belmont, CA: Wadsworth Publishing Company.

Foss, J. S. (2004). *Rhetorical Criticism: Exploration and Practice*. Long Grove, IL: Waveland Press Inc.

DeCasper, A. J., W. P. Fifer. (2008). On human bonding: Newborns prefer their mother's voice. *Science* 208: 1174–1176.

Fredal, J. The language of delivery and the presentation of character: rhetorical action in Demosthenes. (2001). *Rhetorical Review* 20(3/4): 25167.

Golden, J, G. Berquist G, W. Coleman. (2001). *The Rhetoric of Western Thought*. Dubuque, IA: Kendall/Hunt Publishing Company. 12th ed.

Martin Luther King I Have a Dream Speech - American Rhetoric. (n.d.). Retrieved from http://www.americanrhetoric.com/speeches/mlkihaveadream.htm

Theodore Roosevelt, "Duties of American Citizenship." January 26, 1883; Buffalo, New York.

Bacon, Francis. (1955). *Selected Writings of Francis Bacon*.Ed. Hugh G. Dick. New York: Random House Modern Library. p. 230.

Burke, Kenneth. (1945). *A Grammar of Motives*. Berkeley: U of California Press.

Hooks, Bell. (1994). *Teaching to Transgress: Education as the Practice of Freedom.* New York: Routledge, p. 168.

ibid, p. 203

Lyon, Arabella. (1988). "Susanne K. Langer." Retrieved November 2013 from http://eric.ed.gov/?id=ED295157

Nietzsche, Friedrich. Trans. R. J. Hollingdale. (1973). *Beyond Good and Evil.* New York: Penguin Classics, 1990 (first published in 1886).

Nietzsche, Friedrich. Trans. Helen Zimmern. (1997). *Beyond good and evil: Prelude to a philosophy of the future.* New York: Dover Publications, (first published in 1886).

Martin Luther King Jr. (1963). "I Have a Dream" August 28, Washington, D.C.

Check Your Understanding

What is the difference between empiricism and rationalism?

What is postmodernism?

What is epistemology?

What is humanism?

What was unique and especially influential about St. Augustine's use of the art of rhetoric?

What was unique and especially influential about Christine De Pizan?

How did Peter Ramus redefine rhetoric? Explain fully.

"I think, therefore I am" is a reflection of what kind of thinking?

Explain Bacon's faculty of the minds.

Which cannon of delivery become intensely focused on due to Francis Bacon's theories that placed it as a powerful tool?

What is a "nondisputatious model of communication" and who is associated with it?

Who is given some credit for the parting of rhetoric and composition? How did this parting change the ways things are done?

Explain Burkes Dramatis Technique

Explain visual rhetoric as discussed by Sonya K. Foss

What are contemporary ways to establish ethos?

What are contemporary ways to establish pathos?

Who postulated a significant contribution to rhetoric regarding symbolism and meaning during the 19th century? Explain her philosophy.

What was Nietzsche primarily concerned with?

What is visual rhetoric and the three markers of visual rhetoric?

What did Sonya Foss propose as a useful way to evaluate visual imagery? Explain.

Great American Rhetoric Assignment

For this assignment you will need to go online and search the top U.S. speeches in history. Select a speech. If only audio is available that is okay (just not that in the assignment). Listen to the speech once without any interruption and a second time while taking notes and allowing yourself to stop and restart the track or video. Record your reflections regarding the rhetoric here and then use them to type your responses. Answer the following questions fully and with the knowledge you have absorbed thus far in this course. You will turn in a typed version- 12pt font Arial Single spaced 1 page minimum 1 inch margins all the way around.

Speech Title:
Occasion:
Speaker:
Aprox. Date:
Context:

Evaluate the speakers' use of ethos, pathos, and logos.
What was done really well with regard to ethos? Give specific examples.
What was done really well with regard to pathos? Give specific examples.
What was done really well with regard to logos? Give specific examples.
What was the weakest of the three areas - why?
Did the speaker use the classical arrangement set up?
Evaluate the speakers' use of style, delivery, and memory.

4 The Toulmin Model

Chapter Objectives

What is an argument? Stephen Toulmin offered perhaps the best contemporary answer with the development of his eponymous model. Toulmin was a philosopher, logician, and educator. His interest in argumentation was practical and his model reflects his interest in constructing a descriptive model of how people actually argue. Toulmin first proposed his model in the 1958 publication, *The Uses of Argument*. The book has been reprinted fifteen times and remains in print. While he is distinguished in other academic areas, Toulmin's model of argumentation is uniformly considered his most influential work.

Within this chapter, you will learn the Toulmin model. Upon completion of this chapter, you should be able to

- Contrast the Toulmin model with Aristotle's classic model of argumentation
- Name the six components of the Toulmin model
- Distinguish between the three mandatory and three optional parts of the model
- Analyze example arguments based upon the basic Toulmin model

Toulmin Versus Aristotle

The revolutionary nature of the Toulmin model may be illustrated by contrasting Toulmin with Aristotle's classical treatment of argumentation. Aristotle's description of arguments was prescriptive. He was interested in telling others how to argue effectively. As an educator, he taught others how to reason better. His work is theory driven and supported by hypothetical examples. The syllogism was a model that Aristotle invented from his study of logic. It is not a model constructed after listening to how people argue. By following Aristotle's model, students can make arguments that are true, sound, and valid, but they are unlikely to design an argument in the form of a syllogism without first studying Aristotle's work. Syllogisms are not how people typically argue. They are how Aristotle believed that people should argue if they wanted to be effective.

In contrast, Toulmin's model is prescriptive. Toulmin wanted to describe the behavior of people who actually argue, rather than try to construct a model that described some idealized form of argumentation. For years, Toulmin devoted time to researching how people argued. He listened to people debate. He collected research about argumentation. Then, he used all of the information that he amassed to develop his model.

The Components of the Toulmin Model

Toulmin's model identifies six components of an argument: claim, data, warrant, backing, rebuttal, and qualifier. Only the first three parts, the claim, data, and warrant, are required components of every argument. The second set of three, the backing, rebuttal, and qualifier, are optional.

The Mandatory Components

Claim

The **claim** is the conclusion, the end purpose and end point of the argument. The claim is the point that the argument seeks to establish. It describes what the arguer wants to show is true.

Data

The **data** is the evidence used to support the argument. It is the argument's foundation and the basis upon which the argument rests. Data is also the beginning of the argument because it lays the groundwork for the process of argumentation.

Warrant

The warrant is the argument's reasoning. It serves as a connective bridge, linking the data (evidence) to the claim (conclusion). Consider the following example, first in paragraph form:

> We shouldn't sign a treaty with Libya. Libya has broken every single treaty it's signed for the last 50 years. If you can't trust a country to keep its word, you shouldn't be signing treaties with it.

Within this argument, the claim is stated first. The speaker is expressing the view that we ought not sign a treaty with Libya. Then, the evidence is offered second. The data of this argument is the evidence detailing Libya's 50-year history of breaking its treaties. The argument concludes with the warrant connecting the data to the claim.

The Use of Mandatory Components

The claim, data, and warrant are found in every argument, according to Toulmin. However, these three components may be **explicit** or **implicit**. If the component is explicit, it is actually voiced or said. If the component is implicit, then it is unsaid but understood due to the cultural or social framework surrounding the argument. According to Toulmin, it is possible to not state a claim but still make an argument. Similarly, it is possible to not say the warrant or the data and still have an argument.

Toulmin's recognition of implicit and explicit argument components is another factor that distinguishes his model from Aristotle's classical model. Remember that **syllogisms** are, as Aristotle defined them, arguments containing three parts: the major premise, the minor premise, and the conclusion. According to Aristotle, if one of the three parts of a syllogism is missing, then the argument is not a syllogism. Instead, it is an **enthymeme**, which is defined as a syllogism that is not complete. Aristotle regarded enthymemes as defective. If the speaker didn't spell out each of the three parts of the argument, then the speaker was hiding something. The speaker might be ashamed or unreasonable, or otherwise not fully disclosing his motives.

The Optional Components

The Libya argument example does not contain backing, rebuttal, or qualifier. These three items are absent because they are not required for every argument. However, Toulmin observed that they occurred frequently enough in real debates to include within his model as optional components.

Backing

First of all, the **backing** of an argument is the support for the warrant. Backing explains the qualifications or credentials of the warrant. It helps to explain why the warrant is credible. In many cases, the quality of the evidence presented is self-evident or the credibility of the data goes unchallenged. In those cases, backing is not necessary.

Backing is not automatically accepted within an argument. It is possible to have a warrant challenged, to provide backing and to have that backing challenged. The questioning of a debater's source is a common practice and merely stating that the source was published by the *New York Times* or discussed on Fox News does not automatically confer validity to the warrant. If the backing is questioned, the arguer may feel the need to provide additional evidence, or backing, to validate the initial backing.

In the example above, the arguer may have been challenged about the data. A listener might have found it difficult to believe that Libya had not honored a single treaty over a 50-year period. If that objection had occurred, then the argument could have been extended to include backing. The arguer could have explained the source of that information. If pressed for further backing, the arguer could provide additional backing about why that source has sufficient credentials to warrant belief.

Rebuttal

The second optional component of an argument identified by Toulmin is the rebuttal. The **rebuttal** acknowledges that there may be some legitimate limitations or restrictions that can be applied to the argument's claim. As a result, the rebuttal acknowledges those restrictions.

In the Libya example, the arguer may recognize that there are some legitimate restrictions applicable to the argument's claim. If those exist, then the claim could be qualified by the inclusion of a rebuttal. For example, the claim statement could be changed to, "We shouldn't sign a treaty with Libya, unless the country replaces its prime minister."

Qualifier

The sixth and final component of an argument is the qualifier. Qualifiers express the degree of certainty, or modal qualification, that the arguer feels about the claim. Common qualifiers include "probably," "certainly," "necessarily," "presumably," and "impossible." Not every qualifier has the same meaning and some are more rhetorically powerful. Consider the following variations on the Libya example:

Claim without qualifier: We shouldn't sign a treaty with Libya.
Qualifier 1: We probably shouldn't sign a treaty with Libya.
Qualifier 2: We certainly shouldn't sign a treaty with Libya.

Certainly is a more powerful statement of certainty than probably, so the second statement with a qualifier is more forceful than the first. However, the original claim statement without the inclusion qualifier appears more forceful than either statement containing a qualifier. Certainly, the qualifier is optional.

Rebuttals and qualifiers are linked. The inclusion of a rebuttal can create a need to also include a qualifier. After all, rebuttals acknowledge that there may be a legitimate shortcoming or limitation of the claim. Therefore, the claim cannot be concluded with absolute certainty. Similarly, the presence of a qualifier suggests that a legitimate rebuttal does exist. Therefore, when evaluating claims, it is not uncommon to find both a rebuttal and a qualifier within the claim. Within the example, such a claim would look like: We certainly shouldn't sign a treaty with Libya, unless the country replaces its prime minister.

Analyzing Arguments using Toulmin's Model

Toulmin's model may be used to identify the components of an argument and construct visual representations that are useful for analysis. The general diagram of an argument containing just the three mandatory components would look like:

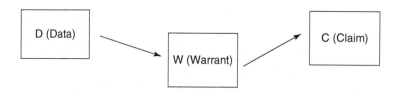

When given a specific argument, you can fill in this basic diagram in order to identify the existing components of the argument. Consider again the following argument:

> We shouldn't sign a peace treaty with Libya. Libya has broken every single treaty it's signed for the last 50 years. If you can't trust a country to keep its word, you shouldn't be signing treaties with it.

From the previous discussion, we already know that this argument contains only the two mandatory components, the data, warrant, and claim. The argument can be drawn to show that the warrant is connecting the data to the claim.

The Toulmin model's visual representation of this argument would look like:

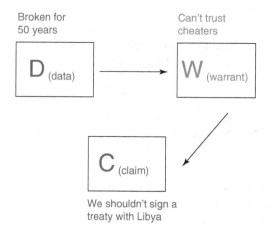

This diagram is relatively simple because the argument contains only the three required components of an argument. Suppose the argument was revised to include the three optional components of an argument:

> We shouldn't sign a peace treaty with Libya. Libya has broken every single treaty it's signed for the last 50 years. The Council for Foreign Relations just released a study, and they are very dead-on in all the country studies that they've done so far, that indicates that Libya has cheated on every treaty for the last 50 years, and you can't trust cheating cheaters in the international realm.

In order to construct a Toulmin model diagram, you should begin by identifying the three mandatory components of the argument. After all, you know that every argument must contain a claim, data, and warrant.

> Main Claim: We shouldn't sign a peace treaty with Libya.
> Data: Libya has broken every single treaty it's signed for the last 50 years.
> Warrant: You can't trust cheating cheaters in the international realm

Once the three mandatory components are identified, you should then look at the rest of the arguments to determine their status.

Additional statements:

1. Council for Foreign Relations just released a study
2. They are very dead-on in all their country studies

These two additional points are not mandatory. They can be omitted and the argument would still be complete. So, you know that the two statements are either backing, qualifier, or rebuttal. You must then use your understanding of these terms to study how they function within the argument to determine their relationship to the data, claim, or warrant.

The complete Toulmin model diagram would look like:

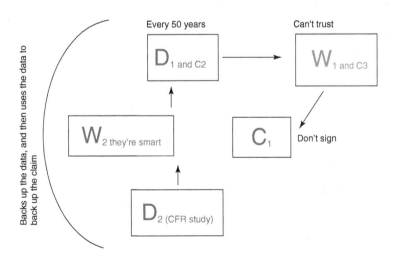

Within this example, both "Council for Foreign Relations just released a study" and "They are very dead-on in all their country studies" are backing up the data.

Informal Logical Fallacies

The logical fallacies in this section are problems with informal reasoning. These are particularly troublesome because each has a germ of truth, each relies on shortcuts of thinking which can prove valuable at times, and each can be defended under certain circumstances. They are counted as logical fallacies because they do not, generally, hold up under careful argumentative scrutiny.

Appeals to Authority and False Authority

We have all encountered this argument. Just recently I was told that I must not support the new healthcare initiative because, "Kim Kardashian says its going to cost a lot of money out of our pockets and let poor people have free insurance while the rest of us have to pay for it ourselves." This is an example of an argument based on a false authority. Who is Kim Kardashian? She is a reality TV star who rose to fame after a scandalous sex video went viral. Is this the definition of a credible authority on national healthcare reform? The answer is clearly a "no."

When we rely on the quotes and reasoning of others to substantiate our own arguments we must be critical of their character and expertise. If they are experts and credible in the field they are discussing they are not usable in argumentation. Similarly, just because some has "Ph.D." after their name doesn't inherently make them credible either. There are many different credentials and each is relevant only depending on the topic at hand. For instance, let's say the authors of this book were asked to discuss a recent trend in argumentation and rhetoric and our evaluation of it. Given that the area is an area of our expertise, we would be considered credible experts. However, if we were asked to discuss the validity of the most recent physics theory, we would not be credible authorities on the subject.

Another way the **appeal to authority** fallacy is used is when someone is considered a credible expert in the field being discussed, but their perspective is offered as evidence that the claim is true instead of recognized as the opinion of one expert, which may not be representative of the entire field of experts. In other words, when citing or quoting an expert who agrees with your claim, make sure your entire claim doesn't rest solely on the opinion of that one person, or you may be committing a fallacy of authority.

> "GarciniaCambogia is currently the best and most natural way to lose weight fast. Dr. Oz says Garcinia Cambogia improves mood, decreases appetite, and results in 4lbs to 15lbs of weight loss per month."

Appeal to Ignorance

The **appeal to ignorance** fallacy occurs when an arguer asks the audience to create an inference based on a premise that is not proven, not provable, or lacks adequate support. Thus, the fallacy basically appeals to the ignorance of the audience. A common fallacy you might have heard is, "No one has proven that ghosts do not exist, therefore they do exist." The appeal is also frequently seen in politics when there has been insufficient research conducted.

In short, the appeal to ignorance argues that because something has not been proven false it is therefore true. It also may argue that something is false purely because it has not been proven to be true.

"Ghosts do not exist because no one has ever proven they exist."

"Immunizations do not cause autism because research hasn't proven that they do."

Red Herring

A **red herring** fallacy occurs when something irrelevant is presented in an attempt to divert the audience's attention from the actual issue at hand. This person will often make an argument that is basically unrelated to the topic, but just slightly connected in an attempt to get you thinking about that new (often emotion-evoking) issue and thus forget to argue the point at hand. They are primarily changing the topic.

> *"We agree that the issue of gays and lesbians having the right to marry is important. But, I also see that there are so many important issues to vote on and discuss right now that it's overwhelming and getting out of hand."*

Appeal to Fear

One of the most common types of fallacies you see on television is the **appeal to fear,** which really means that someone is using a scare tactic. Using an appeal to fear means the arguer is triggering a fear response from the audience in order to get them to believe their claims. Humans are quite susceptible to fear tactics. For some reason it is just so much easier to accept a devastating possibility than to question the statistical likelihood of the idea.

> *"Recently three women have been attacked in their homes in various locations on the west side of town. Therefore, those of you living on the west side should stay locked indoors and make sure you have a defense device armed should you leave."*

Personal Attacks, also Known as "Ad Hominem"

An **ad hominem** fallacy occurs when an arguer attacks someone personally rather than the argument itself. Argumentation should always be directed at the logic and reasoning, not at the people progressing them, straying from this ideal results in a personal attack fallacy. You have endlessly endured these fallacies in political conversations. Former President of the United States Bill Clinton is still criticized for his affair with Monica Lewinsky when his policies are debated. His womanizing ways are not what the debate is about, bringing up sexual history when discussing the effectiveness of his foreign policy qualifies as a personal attack, not a legitimate argument.

> *Jerome: "I gave you three reasons and three pieces of supporting evidence as to why abortion should be legal in the first trimester. I believe those abortions should remain legal."*
>
> *Skylar: "Of course you do, you're an atheist who doesn't believe in God, the commandments, and has no real appreciation for life."*
>
> *Jerome: "My being an atheist has nothing to do with this. My arguments were presented and evidence to back up my ideas given, that is what we are talking about."*
>
> *Skylar: "It doesn't matter what your reasoning is, if you are not religious you wouldn't understand."*

Hypocrite, also Known as "Ad Hominem Tu Quoque"

Ad hominem tu quoque is a kind of personal attack where the arguer doesn't just attack the person specifically at random, but does so because it points out an inconsistency in their arguments. The hypocrite fallacy is called such because it points out that person's arguments are inconsistent with their actions.

> *"Doing drugs like marijuana is bad and should be illegal. Marijuana is more harmful to your lungs than cigarette smoking. In fact, according to studies, smoking one marijuana joint is the same as smoking 3 to 24 cigarettes."*

> *Sam: "Do you smoke marijuana?"*

> *Beth: "Yes, on occasion."*

> *Sam: "You're a hypocrite!"*

Appeal to Tradition

An **appeal to tradition** fallacy occurs when it is argued that because something has been done in the past, is older, historical, or tradition it is therefore better or the best. This type of reasoning is problematic because age alone does not determine the legitimacy of something. Because people like their traditions they are likely to use this fallacy. We tend to stick with things we know because they are comfortable, safe, and predictable. But the idea that just because something is older or done more often in the past is inherently right is wrong and illogical.

> *"I have to believe in God. God and the bible have existed for centuries. The story of God and his teaching have been around for thousands of years so it must be true."*

> *"Traditionally the idea of marriage has been operationalized as a man and a woman committed to one another. It has always been that way and it should remain that way."*

Straw Man Fallacy

The **straw man** fallacy occurs when an arguer represents the opponent's position by presenting it as a weaker version than it really is, in an effort to more easily knock it down. Straw man fallacies are performed with a substitution of distorted, exaggerated, or misrepresented versions of the actual opposition argument.

> *"The congressman supports shutting down the nuclear weapons budget for one year, but I can't see why anyone would want to completely dismantle the United States' ability to defend itself."*

Conclusion

British philosopher and logician Stephen Toulmin created a six-part model of argumentation based upon his empiric observation of real-life arguments. Based upon his observations, Toulmin identified three required components found in every argument. The claim is the conclusion of the argument and the point that the argument is attempting to show as true. The data is the evidence that serves as the foundation of the argument. The warrant is the reasoning of the argument that connects the claim to the data.

Toulmin's model also recognizes the existence of three optional components. First, the backing is the qualifications or credentials of the warrant. Backing is not automatically accepted within an argument and it is possible to provide backing for backing to satisfy the skepticism of an arguer. Second, the rebuttal acknowledges that there may be some legitimate limitations or restrictions that can be applied to the argument's claim. Finally, the qualifier expresses the degree of certainty, or modal qualification, that the arguer feels about the claim. If the speaker is not totally certain that the claim is true, then the statement of the claim will likely contain a qualifier such as "probably" or "likely."

Toulmin's model may be distinguished from Aristotle's classical model of argumentation in at least two substantial ways. First of all, Aristotle's model was prescriptive and Toulmin's was descriptive. Aristotle was interested in constructing good arguments and teaching people how to make arguments that are sound, valid, and true. In contrast, Toulmin's model is based upon practice and research, rather than theory. Toulmin didn't want to develop the perfect argument model. Instead, he wanted to develop a model that accurately described arguments as they occur in real life.

In addition, Toulmin acknowledged the existence of explicit and implicit components of an argument. Explicit components are spoken by the arguer. Implicit components are unspoken. However, the surrounding cultural environment permits the acknowledgement of the unstated part of the argument. In contrast, Aristotle's classical model of an argument does not tolerate missing parts. A syllogism must contain a major premise, a minor premise, and a conclusion or it ceases to be a syllogism and instead becomes an enthymeme.

The Toulmin model can be used to analyze arguments. Knowledge of the parts of the Toulmin model permits the individual to identify and map the components of any argument.

Key Terms

Backing—Within the Toulmin model, the qualifications or credentials of the warrant and an optional component of an argument

Claim—Within the Toulmin model, the conclusion of the argument and a mandatory component of every argument

Data—Within the Toulmin model, the evidence and foundation for the argument and a mandatory component of every argument

Enthymeme—According to Aristotle, a defective syllogism that is missing at least one of its three required components

Explicit—The stated parts of an argument

Implicit—The unstated parts of an argument that are still acknowledged due to the surrounding cultural or social framework

Qualifier—Within the Toulmin model, the qualifier expresses the degree of certainty, or modal qualification, that the arguer feels about the claim. Examples include the words "certainly," "probably," "never," and "definitely"

Rebuttal—Within the Toulmin model, the acknowledgement that there may be legitimate limitations placed upon the argument's claim and an optional component of an argument.

Syllogism—According to Aristotle, an argument containing a major premise, a minor premise, and a conclusion

Warrant—Within the Toulmin model, the reasoning of the argument and a mandatory component of every argument

Check Your Understanding

List and explain the six components of an argument according to the Toulmin Model.

1.

2.

3.

4.

5.

6.

Given the Toulmin Model, create an argument of your choosing. Label each part then provide your example. This may require that you do some minimal research.

1.

2.

3.

4.

5.

6.

Name the eight informal logical fallacies discussed in your chapter and describe them briefly.

1.

2.

3.

4.

5.

6.

7.

8.

Provide an example (not from your book) of each of the eight informal logical fallacies.

1.

2.

3.

4.

5.

6.

7.

8.

Toulmin Model Mapping

This page should help you craft stronger arguments. Map out 2 arguments you plan to progress in an upcoming debate using this simplified mapping.

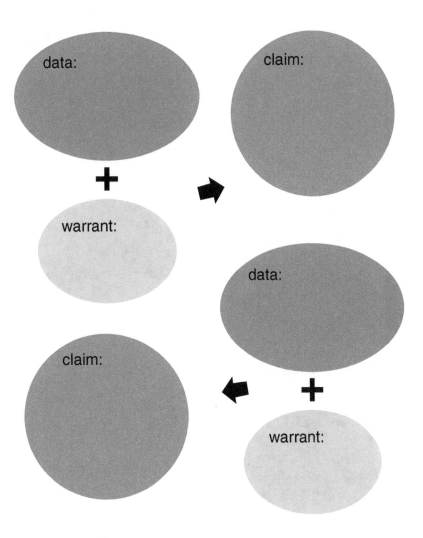

5 The Deductive Model

Chapter Objectives

Human beings possess the extraordinary ability to consciously collect data, apply logic, verify knowledge and form conclusion, a characteristic known as reason. Reason is closely associated with the concepts of cognition, intelligence and thought. Reason enables human beings to understand the world around them by recognizing features such as truth, falsehood, cause and effect.

Reasoning is classically divided into two categories or models: deductive and inductive. This chapter explores the logical reasoning methods known as deductive reasoning. The next chapter will then discuss inductive reasoning. Practically, human beings use both deductive and inductive reasoning. They will move from one type of reasoning to the other as the circumstances and available knowledge dictates. However, it is still useful to learn about deductive and inductive reasoning separately, to learn about their key differences and how those structural differences impact the certainty of their conclusions.

Within this chapter, you will learn to identify and apply deductive reasoning. The chapter is divided into four sections. The first section discusses formal logic, which is the organized study of reasoning, the definition and form of deductive arguments, and the three major characteristics of deductive arguments: truth, validity and soundness. The second section discusses two specific forms of deductive reasoning, the syllogism and the enthymeme. The third section then introduces a common tool for deduction: Venn diagrams. The final section presents common forms of deductive fallacies.

Formal Logic

Formal logic is the structured study of reasoning. Formal logic is a mechanism used to evaluate the components of reasoning. It is important to remember that formal logic focuses upon the form of the argument, not the specific content of the propositions found within the argument. This distinction will become more apparent later in this chapter.

Deductive reasoning moves from the consideration of the general to a greater understanding of the specific. Deductive reasoning has several names. It is also known as deductive logic, logical deduction and top-down logic.

Deductive reasoning is distinguished from inductive reasoning by its claim to establish the certainty of its conclusion. If the components of a deductive argument are true and the rules of logic are applied correctly, then the conclusion of a deductive argument is **necessarily true**. Necessity is a philosophical concept which captures the idea that something must be so: it is not merely that a proposition is the case, or even that we are certain that it is so, but that the statement must be the case. In contrast, inductive arguments do not claim to offer proof that a claim is certainly, much less necessarily, true. Instead, the outcome of an inductive argument is probable.

Arguments and Propositions

An **argument** is a set of statements, one of which serves as a conclusion, while the others together provide support for that conclusion. This concept of argument goes back to Aristotle, about 2,500 years ago, who defined these structures of thought in the invention of logic. Aristotle came to understand that thoughts could be organized in ways that let us more effectively understand ourselves and the world. Arguments have been a critically important part of how persons have come to understand the world ever since.

One way to understand arguments is as structured text. Arguments can be expressed in many ways: spoken or displayed on a computer screen using a human language, presented as logical symbols in a formal language, or even performed in a kinesthetic dance. Arguments are often expressed as structured text in a specific language, so let us consider arguments presented in that form. Not just any set of sounds or marks, words, pictures, ideas or propositions qualify as an argument. The sequence of words must have the right structure to qualify as an argument. Understanding that text is structured is the first step here.

Some sequences of sounds are words and some are not. In English, for example, the sounds represented by "lulilula" are not structured to form a word, while the sounds represented by "obstreperous" are. Similarly, some sequences of words are sentences and some are not. In English, for example, the sequence of words "Running running click sunset dreams." is not structured correctly to form an acceptable sentence, while the words in "Werewolf zombies would be formidable if they kept their werewolf abilities." Finally, some sequences of sentences are arguments and some are not. For example, the following sequences of statements are not reasonably understood as forming an argument: "Today is Sunday. My name is Michael. Thus, sunscreens do prevent skin cancer." Although the individual symbols are structured correctly to form words in English, and the words are organized in an appropriate way to construct valid sentences, the statements are not structured appropriately to form an argument. Contrast the previous example with the following argument: "All Greeks are mortal. Socrates is a Greek. Therefore, Socrates is mortal." The last example is text structured appropriately to express an argument. Aristotle understood that a set of statements organized such that one serves as a conclusion while the others support it expressed something very valuable, an argument.

Arguments are composed of a series of propositions. A **proposition** is a declarative statement in a language which is either true or false. While it is possible for an individual to not know if a proposition is true or false, it must be one or the other. Some statements cannot be regarded as propositions because they are not clearly true or false. For example, statements about ethics, whether something is right or wrong, beautiful or ugly, are likely to require further judgment and cannot therefore be propositions.

Simple propositions are made up of a subject and a predicate. You are likely to be familiar with these terms from your English grammar lessons. The subject of a proposition is a noun and details what the statement is about. The subject is typically the first part of the sentence but this is not always the case. The predicate of a proposition is what is said about the subject. The predicate of a proposition is usually, but not always, the latter portion of the statement, and the predicate will typically begin with a verb.

Consider the following proposition:

"My name is Eloise."

This statement is a proposition because it is a statement which can be true or false. Either the speaker's name is Eloise or it is not. The subject of this proposition is "My name." The predicate of this proposition is "is Eloise."

Here is another example:

"Today is the 24th of July."

Again, this statement is a proposition because it is either true or false. As a reader of the statement, you can check the calendar to determine the truth of the statement. The subject of this proposition is "Today."

The predicate begins with the verb "is." The complete predicate is "is the 24th of July."

Truth

As the previous section indicated, truth is a property of propositions or statements. Deductive reasoning, if conducted in a logical manner, claims absolute certainty and the conclusion of a deductive argument is necessarily true. The significance of truth in distinguishing between a deductive reasoning and inductive reasoning warrants further consideration. One says of a proposition or statement that it is TRUE if it is the case. One says of a proposition or statement that it is FALSE if it is not the case. In other words, truth is the opposite of falsehood.

A proposition is a type of truthbearer. A **truthbearer** is something which can be true or false. Propositions are not the only kind of truthbearer. Statements, beliefs and utterance may also be truthbearers.

A truthbearer must be true or false. A **truthmaker** aids in the determination of whether a truthbearer is true or false. Facts, events, states of affairs, cases and other types of evidence can act as truthmakers. In the right structure, many things could be truthmakers.

Theories of Truth

The nature of truth is debated vigorously by philosophers and academic scholars, who disagree on the standards or rules that should be applied to determine the truth of statements. Their disagreement leads to different theories and criteria for truth. A theory of truth is an explanation of how truth works: they typically identify truthbearers and truthmakers and their interaction. This section discusses the six major theories of truth.

First of all, subjective theories of truth depend upon individual perception. They maintain that truth is decided by the subject considering a given proposition, determined by the feelings, observations and beliefs of the individual. Understood simply, subjective theories of truth believe that something is true if a person believes that it is true and other's conclusions, evidence, or arguments only matter insofar as they influence the subject's evaluation.

For example, Sarah-Jane believes in guardian angels. She attributes her recent survival in a serious car accident to the intervention of her own personal guardian angel. Subjective theories of truth contend that the existence of a guardian angel must be true because the individual believes that it is true. So, according to subjective theories of truth, Sarah-Jane's guardian angel exists. Therefore, others cannot disprove the existence of her guardian angel.

Within postmodern society, subjective theories of truth may initially seem appealing. However, there is a basic problem: reality can trump the truth of subjective claims. For example, a person may believe that they can fly. However, when they jump out of a window, they quickly learn that they were incorrect. Belief in their ability to fly did not make it true.

Social/consensual theories of truth are closely related to subjective theories but expand the conception of truth to consider the perception of large groups. Something is true if a group of persons believe that it is true. To some extent, social/consensual theories of truth are stricter in their definition of truth than subjective theories. After all, subjective theories of truth rely upon the perception of just one person. In contrast, social/consensual theories require the development of a consensus. Virtually everyone within the group has to share a belief before it can be declared true.

For example, almost everyone believes that Neil Armstrong was the first man to walk on the moon. Very few people disagree with this claim. Therefore, the claim that Neil Armstrong was the first man to walk on the moon may be considered true.

However, like subjective theories of truth, social/consensual theories are problematic. Beliefs developed through consensus have been proven empirically false. For example, the consensus was once that the world was flat and was the center of the universe. However, collected evidence has since proven that the world is not flat and that the planet is not the center of the universe. The consensus has changed over time because the previous consensus was incorrect.

The third collection of truth theories are social-constructivist in nature. They argue that truth is constructed, just like the rest of reality. As a result, there is no real. Truth is all in our heads.

The social-constructivist theory of truth can be examined in the context of the definition of marriage. The tradition view of marriage is that it is an institution joining one man to one woman. That idea of marriage was made that way. The definition of marriage is gradually being changed to include unions that do not include one man and one woman.

Social-constructivist theories of truth are vulnerable to the same problems as the subjective and social/consensual theories. Human perception is limited and beliefs derived from that limited perception can be incorrect. Furthermore, large portions of reality existed before the existence of human beings. Those portions of reality would continue to exist even if human beings had never come into being.

Fourth, verificationist theories of truth focus upon what can be proven with evidence. Something is considered true if it is proven true with evidence. That truth will continue to be truth until proven otherwise. Weaker versions of verificationist theories will consider a statement to be potentially true or potentially false based upon the ability to verify, or prove the conclusion true.

For example, the statement that climate change is man-made is true. It is true because scientists have accumulated a great deal of evidence showing that it is true. However, it is possible that sufficient evidence could be collected to make the claim that climate change is man-made false.

Verificationist theories of truth are problematic because there are things that are true which cannot be proven and things that are false which cannot be disproven. For example, the legal system in the United States uses evidence to determine whether an individual is guilty or innocent of a crime. However, sometime the evidence is insufficient. A person who did not commit a crime may be found guilty. A person who did commit a crime may be acquitted. These determinations are truth dependent upon the evidence available and their determinations may not accurately reflect what actually happened.

Coherence theories of truth require what is believed to be true to fit within the broader tapestry of belief. Individuals believe many different things to be true. Truth is regarded as a part of that broader belief system. Coherence occurs when a belief, if true, is consistent with other beliefs also believed to be true. Something can only be true if it fits into the web of the rest of one's beliefs.

The example of evolution illustrates the primary shortcoming of coherentist theories. Half of the population of the United States does not believe that evolution is true. They reject the truth of evolution because it conflicts with their religious views, which they believe to be true. Because evolution contradicts what they believe, they treat evolution as false, despite the evidence supporting it to be true.

The Correspondence Theory of Truth maintains that the truth of a statement is dependent upon its agreement with reality. A Correspondence Theory of Truth was first articulated by Aristotle in his Metaphysics. This most ancient theory of truth is simply stated: a proposition is true if it corresponds with the facts. This theory is a common-sense understanding of truth. For example, if you were to say "It's snowing outside right now." we would conclude that your claim was true if and only if it was, in fact, snowing outside at that moment and would conclude that it was false if it was not. Correspondence theory is also the received view among philosophers.

For a Correspondence Theory of Truth, the truth bearers are propositions and the truth makers are facts. These theories posit a direct relationship between reality and propositions: our beliefs and their popularity, the evidence for and against those beliefs, and whether those beliefs fit comfortably with our understanding of the world have nothing to do with it. For a proposition to be true, it must correspond to the facts.

Finally, semantic theory is a specialized version of the Correspondence Theory of Truth. Semantic theory maintains that a property of sentences is truth. It takes the form: "P" is true if and only if P.

For example, consider the statement:

"Today is Tuesday"

This statement is true if and only if today is Tuesday.

Although the Correspondence Theory of Truth and Semantic Theories have withstood against the best arguments marshalled against them, they do have weaknesses. Specifically, both theories struggle to accurately account for imaginary and fictional entities. For example, nearly everyone considers that the statements "Superman wears a red cape." and "Unicorns have a single horn protruding from their foreheads" are true. However, since Superman and unicorns do not actually exist, there are no facts in reality for those propositions to correspond to. This is a problem for the Correspondence Theory of Truth and its Semantic variants. Philosophers have provided a couple of solutions to these and related problems, but even our most time-tested and common-sense theory of truth isn't without issues.

Characteristics of Arguments
Validity

Validity is a property of arguments and only arguments. An argument is valid if and only if the reasoning in it is good. If the reasoning is deficient, then the argument is invalid. Propositions do not have this property and so cannot be said to be valid or invalid.

The validity of an argument does not depend upon whether its premises are true. To assess the validity of an argument, one should assume that the premises are true and then see if the conclusion MUST be true. If the conclusion must be true, then the argument is valid. If the conclusion could still be false, then the argument is invalid.

Consider the following:

> All Greeks are males.
> Aristotle is a Greek.
> Therefore, Aristotle is a male.

Is this a valid argument?

The correct answer is yes, this is a valid argument. However, you may have initially believed that this argument is not valid. After all, all Greeks are not male. Some Greeks are female. However, this objection focuses upon the truth of the premises, not the reasoning of the argument.

In fact, this is a valid argument even though the first premise is false. Validity has nothing to do with the facts or the veracity of the premises. Rather, validity concentrates upon the reasoning in the argument. Assuming that the premises of the argument are true, it is both certain and necessary that Aristotle is a male, and the argument is therefore valid.

Now, consider another argument:

> All Greeks are male.
> Socrates is male.
> Socrates is Greek.

Is this argument valid?

The preceding example is invalid. If the first two lines are assumed to be true, the conclusion is not necessarily true. As a male, Socrates could be a Greek. However, it is also possible for Socrates to not be Greek. Socrates could be Italian or French. All Greeks are male but not all males are Greek. Since it is possible for the conclusion to be false even when the premises are true, the argument is invalid.

The formal test of validity proceeds in 3 steps. Firstly, one must assume that the premises of the argument are true. Secondly, one considers whether the conclusion of the argument must be true, given the truth of the premises. Finally, one decides that the argument is valid if and only if the conclusion must be true and that the argument is invalid if the conclusion could nonetheless be false. This formal test of the validity of an argument specifies what it means for the logic and reasoning in an argument to be "solid."

Step 1: Assume the Premises
Step 2: Assess the Conclusion
Step 3: Decide on Validity

Soundness

Like validity, soundness is a property of arguments. Just like validity, soundness is only a property of arguments. Propositions do not have this property and cannot be said to be sound or not sound.

Soundness exists if a given argument is valid and if its premises are true. To be sound, an argument must be valid: the reasoning of an argument has to be solid for it to be sound. But validity is insufficient for the soundness of an argument, the argument's premises must also be true. Those valid arguments with one or more false premises are not sound: even though the reasoning in those arguments is solid, the argument as a whole fails because it relies on false premises.

Consider the following example of a valid argument with false premises:

All Greeks are males.
Aristotle is a Greek.
Therefore, Aristotle is a male.

From the last section, we know that this argument is valid because if the premises are assumed to be true, then the conclusion must be true. However, this argument is not sound because the premises are not true. We know that not all Greeks are males because some Greeks exist who are females. Therefore, while the argument is valid, it does not have premises that are true, and so it does not have the property of soundness.

Similarly, an argument with true premises and a true conclusion can be unsound because it is invalid. Consider the following example of an invalid argument with true premises:

All cardinals are red.
Jupiter is a planet.
Therefore, soccer is the world's most popular sport.

In this example, each proposition is true, but the argument is invalid and therefore unsound. Even though all cardinals are red and Jupiter is a planet, those do not necessitate that soccer is the world's most popular sport: the conclusion could, nonetheless, be false.

Syllogisms & Enthymemes

Aristotle first identified the structure of a syllogism over 2,000 years ago. This most ancient form of argument, together with its malformed sibling, the enthymeme, dominated western thought about reason and rationality for 2 millennia. That is 2,000 years in which to be rational, a thinker essentially needed to have mastered syllogisms.

This section begins with a discussion of the definition of syllogisms and the dissection of a syllogism into its constituent parts.

Syllogisms

Syllogisms are, as Aristotle defined them, arguments with three parts, one of which is the conclusion and the other two the premises which support that conclusion. The two premises of a syllogism are further distinguished into the major premise and the minor premise. Aristotle invented logic in his creation and examination of the syllogism. By treating these kinds of arguments as objects of study and then actually studying them, Aristotle became the first person we know of to systemically examine forms of thinking.

In a normal-form syllogism, the **major premise** is stated first. However, syllogisms are not always in the normal form. If a statement in the syllogism contains a quantifier or conditional, it is likely to the major premise. Common quantifiers found within a major premise include all, every, no, and some. Common conditionals include, if then, in case of, either or, and when. The major premise is the premise containing the major term and the middle term of the syllogism.

In contrast, the **minor premise** is the premise containing the minor term and the middle term. In normal form, the minor premise is the second premise of the syllogism. In addition, the subject of the minor premise is often a specific person or particular case or subset.

The conclusion contains the major term and the minor term of the syllogism. It is the part of the syllogism typically offered last. The conclusion can also be described as the point that the syllogism is attempting to prove.

The Three Parts of Every Syllogism:

1. Major Premise   MP   All Greeks are men.
2. Minor Premise   mp   Socrates is a Greek.
3. Conclusion   C   Socrates is a man.

Syllogisms have also traditionally been dissected into the 3 terms which are typically present. The 3 terms are the major term, middle term, and minor term. The **major term** is the predicate of the major premise and of the conclusion. The **minor term** is the subject of the minor premise and the conclusion. The **middle term** appears in both of the premises but not the conclusion. These terms provide a clear way to distinguish the major and minor premise besides order.

Types of Syllogisms

Different kinds of syllogisms exist. A **categorical syllogism** is defined by the existence of a major premise that admits no exceptions or conditions. The major premise will contain exclusionary language to this effect. Terms such as like, all, every, or no within the major premise identify the categorical syllogism.

Example:

(MP):	All X are Y
(mp)	A is an X
(C)	A is a Y

All dogs are mammals.
Cornell is a dog.
Cornell is a mammal.

In a **disjunctive syllogism**, the major premise forces a choice between competing premises and mutual alternatives. The major premise in a disjunctive syllogism has language like "not both," "either or but not both" or "if then not" language. There are 2 different kinds of disjunctive syllogism that seem very similar: one type states that one of the alternatives will occur but not both alternatives ("Either X or Y but not both") and the other type just states that not both alternatives will occur ("Not both X and Y").

Example 1:

(MP)	Either X or Y but not both
(mp)	X
(C)	not Y

Example 2:

(MP)	Not both X and Y
(mp)	X
(C)	not Y

A third type of syllogism is the **hypothetical syllogism**. In a hypothetical syllogism, the major premise is a hypothetical or conditional statement. The major premise in a hypothetical syllogism contains hypothetical or conditional language like "if, then" "When, then" or "in case, then."

Example:

(MP)	If X then Y
(mp)	X
(C)	Y

The above structure has a proper name: Modus Ponens. Modus Ponens has been called the deep structure underlying all arguments. This meaning will become more evident in the later section on truth tables.

A textual example of a hypothetical syllogism:

If it rains, the car seat will get wet.
It is raining.
The car seat will get wet.

Enthymemes

The definition of an enthymeme is a contested subject. Traditionally, the enthymeme is a syllogism with one of the 3 parts missing. For example, an enthymeme may contain a major premise and a conclusion, but no minor premise. Alternatively, an enthymeme may contain a major premise and a minor premise but lack a conclusion. Some scholars of Aristotle argue that he might have intended an enthymeme to refer to any defective syllogism.

Enthymemes can be repaired in order to create a syllogism. This process begins by examining an argument to determine whether it is a syllogism or an enthymeme. If it is an enthymeme, the existing parts should be identified in order to determine which of the three component parts of the syllogism is absent. Then, the missing component should be supplied in order to create the syllogism.

Venn Diagrams

A **Venn diagram** is a visual aid that shows the possible logical relationships between a limited collection of sets. Venn diagrams are a way to visual sets and logical relationships between them. John Venn formalized what are now known as Venn diagrams in 1880 as a visual method of working through ideas in logic and set theory. For centuries, Venn diagrams were used casually. However, Venn formalized their use for set theory and logic and his work attached his name to what is also known as a set diagram.

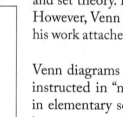

Venn diagrams are used in many fields of education. Students instructed in "new math" were presented with Venn diagrams in elementary school. Venn diagrams are also used by students in computer science, linguistics and statistics. Venn diagrams are useful in logic as a tool to graphically depict categorical and disjunctive syllogisms.

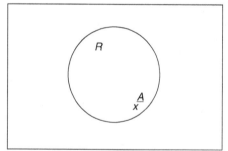

The model of a Venn diagram is relatively simple. A box represents the space of ALL, or at least the space of ALL for a given domain. Within the box, we draw regions or circles to represent subsets of ALL and position individual and particular members appropriately. With a regular set of rules, we can visualize categorical relationships and interactions.

This is the box of ALL. Inside the box is everything. One may be tempted to say that nothing is outside the box, but that is incorrect: even nothing is inside the box.

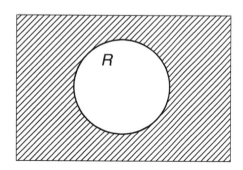

Five basic Venn diagrams are useful to evaluate relationships. The first is membership. To illustrate that A is a member of the set R, we draw a closed region to represent the set R and then put a locating x (like "x marks the spot" on a pirate map) labeled with an "A" within R. This Venn diagram could represent: Andy is Rich, that argyle sweater is ripped, Alien was directed by Ridley Scott, and so on. Generally, speaking any relationship such that **A** ∈ **R** (the item A is a member of the set R).

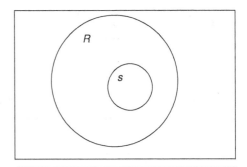

The second Venn diagram is negation. To illustrate the set of all things which are not in the set R, we shade the entire region outside of R. The shaded region is the set of all things variously not rich, or not ripped, or not directed by Ridley Scott. Generally speaking, it is ~**R** (all that is not in the set R).

The third use for the Venn Diagram is containment. To illustrate that the set S is contained in the set R, we draw a region representing S fully inside the region representing the set R. This Venn diagram could represent: every snake is a reptile, all sauces are rich, scanty swimsuits are racy, and so on. Generally, speaking any relationship such that **S** ⊂ **R** (the set S is contained by the set R). Logically, it is implication, if S then R.

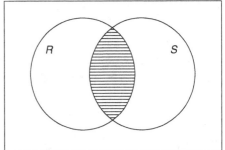

Intersection shows that some sets share members. To illustrate the set of members of both sets R and S, we shade the region that is shared by both sets R and S. This Venn diagram could represent: the set of rich and short people, the snakes that are red, or all sandy beaches in Romania. Generally speaking that region is the intersection of the sets S and R, notated as S ∩ R. Logically, it is the conjunction, S and R, also noted as S ∧ R.

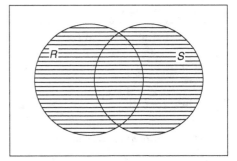

The final illustration is union. To illustrate the set of members of either set R or set S, we shade the region that has members of set R or of set S or of both. This Venn diagram could represent: anyone who is rich or short, all things that are either silver or red, or all warriors who were samurai or ronin. Generally speaking that region is the union of the sets S and R, notated as S ∪ R. Logically, it is the disjunction, S or R, also noted as S ∨ R.

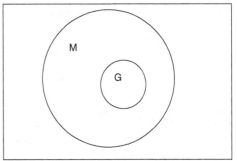

The use of a Venn diagram to evaluate a syllogism involves three steps. Consider the following example syllogism:

(MP)   All Greeks are Mortal
(mp)   Socrates is a Greek
(C)   Socrates is a Mortal

The first step is to draw the major premise. The major premise in the example states that all Greeks (G) belong to or are in M (Mortal).

That seems to be a containment relationship.

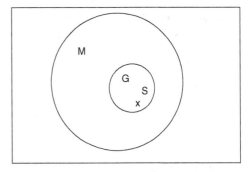

Then, the second step involves drawing the minor premise. This minor premise states that S (Socrates) is a member of or kind of G (Greek).

That is a membership relationship.

The resultant Venn diagram must be inspected to determine if the conclusion is necessarily so. It is. There is no way to draw the diagram to make Socrates a Greek without him also being a moral if all Greeks are mortal. Therefore, the Venn diagram shows that the syllogism is valid.

Logical Fallacies

Deductive logical fallacies are always invalid arguments. Moreover, many of them appear to be valid arguments and those untrained in logic can easily be fooled by them. As is often the case, the best defense is by understanding when they are being attempted. This section provides a brief list of the deductive fallacies you are most likely to encounter: affirming the consequent, denying the antecedent, equivocation, division, accident, and false dichotomy.

Affirming the Consequent

The fallacy of **affirming the consequent** occurs when a premise associates one particular instance to an entire consequent or result. Affirming the consequent can be represented this way:

> **If P then Q**
> **Q**
> **Therefore, P**

> *If Oprah owns a castle she is rich.*
> *Oprah is rich.*
> *Therefore, Oprah owns a castle*

> *If Monty has an ear infection, then he has a fever*
> *Monty has a fever*
> *Therefore, Monty has an ear infection*

Denying the Antecedent

The fallacy of **denying the antecedent** happens when the minor premise asserts that the antecedent does not obtain. A statement that has the "If P then Q" form is called a conditional statement. P is the antecedent and Q is the consequent of the conditional statement. Arguments that deny the antecedent are invalid because their conclusions do not necessarily follow from the premises. Denying the antecedent can be understood this way:

> **If P then Q**
> **Not P**
> **So, not Q**

> *If you smoke cigarettes you will get lung cancer.*
> *You don't smoke cigarettes.*
> *Therefore, you won't get lung cancer.*

If they are not sweating, touching their mouths, and fighting they are telling the truth.
They are sweating, touching their mouths, and fighting.
So, they are not telling the truth.

Equivocation

The fallacy of **equivocation** occurs when the arguer uses a word that has two different meanings in their arguments. For instance, the word "bank" could mean the place you keep your money and get loans from. The word "bank" could also refer to the edge of a river.

The fraternity I want to rush has mostly kids that are rich.
My teacher told me I am rich in all the ways that matter in life.
I should rush and be admitted into that fraternity.

Division

The **division** fallacy occurs when the major premise of a deductive argument is concerned with characteristics that apply to a group as a whole, and cannot be "divided" and applied to specific cases.
Small businesses are shutting down at a rapid pace.
My mom owns a small business.
My mom is shutting down at rapid pace.

Accident

The accident fallacy is an interesting one, because just the name itself seems to imply that it was unintentionally illogical, when this is most likely not the case. The accident fallacy occurs when an arguer claims that a rule is applied to something that it really does not apply to. In other words, A is understood by the rule of Z. But, A doesn't actually fall under the rule of Z.

"Coach you can't go in the locker room, only athletes are allowed in the locker room."
"You should not have shot that intruder, killing is bad."

False Dichotomy also known as the Either-or Fallacy

Another common fallacy you see on TV, in your homes, and especially in political campaigns, is the false dichotomy or "either-or" fallacy. In the **false dichotomy** fallacy the arguer craftily misrepresents the number of options available to the audience. There are two options provided to an audience and usually one is clearly painted in a positive way and the alternative choice is awful, frightening, or completely unimaginable.

For example, you may have been told that, "If you don't vote Democrat, you vote Republican." This statement is not entirely true. There are more options out there, you could vote Libertarian, Independent, for the Peace and Freedom Party and many others. There are more options, but the arguer does not want you to think of them, they merely want you to think about how much you would never vote Republican.

Just think back to your childhood for a moment, you were sitting down to eat your meal and your father placed a large scoop of peas next to your potatoes and chicken. You refused to eat them, and so he said, "You either eat your peas, or spend the rest of the night in your room." You see; either- or fallacies are everywhere!

"Either we increase the punishments for drug use and distribution or we accept defeat and legalize it."

Conclusion

This chapter introduced deduction, one of the two types of reasoning. Deductive reasoning moves from the consideration of the general to the identification of the specific, resulting in a certain conclusion. Formal logic, the study of reasoning, identifies arguments as a series of propositions, or declarative statements, that support a conclusion. The characteristics of arguments include truth, validity and soundness.

Syllogisms are deductive arguments with three parts, one of which is the conclusion and the other two the premises that support the conclusion. The three major types of syllogisms are distinguished by features of the major premise. Categorical syllogisms contain a major premise that admits no exception or condition. Disjunctive syllogisms for a choice between exclusive alternatives within the major premise. Hypothetical syllogisms feature hypothetical or conditional statements as the major premise. Enthymemes are faulty syllogisms generally missing one of the three required components.

Tools for deduction include the Venn diagram and truth tables. These tools can be used to test an argument.

Key Terms

Argument—A set of statements, one of which serves as a conclusion, while the others together provide support for that conclusion.

Categorical Syllogism—A syllogism containing a major premise that admits no exceptions or conditions.

Conclusion—Within a syllogism, the conclusion is the statement containing the major term and the minor term.

Deductive reasoning—The process of reasoning that moves from the general to the specific

Disjunctive Syllogism—A syllogism containing a major premise that forces a choice between competing premises and mutual alternatives.

Enthymeme—A faulty syllogism generally missing one of the three required components

Formal Logic—The study of deductive arguments and the propositions found within those arguments, concentrating upon form rather than substance

Hypothetical Syllogism—A syllogism in which the major premise is a conditional or hypothetical statement.

Necessarily True—Logical Truth

Major Premise—The premise in a syllogism containing the major term and the middle term, as well as any qualifiers/quantifiers. Also, the first premise offered in the normal form of a syllogism.

Major Term—In a syllogism, the major term is the predicate of the conclusion and the predicate in the major premise.

Minor Premise—The premise in a syllogism containing the minor term and the middle term, in normal form.

Minor Term—In a syllogism, the minor term is the subject of the minor premise and the subject of the conclusion.

Proposition—A declarative statement in a language, composed of a subject and a predicate, that is either true or false

Soundness—A property of arguments; an argument is sound if and only if it is both valid and all of its premises are true.

Syllogism—An argument composed of three parts: the major premise, the minor premise and the conclusion.

Truth—a property of propositions or statements; if it is the case, then it is true.

Truth Table—compound propositions made up of two or more propositions joined by a connector.

Truthbearer—Something which can be true or false

Truthmaker—Something which determines whether a truthbearer is true or false

Validity—A property of an argument: an argument is valid if and only if the reasoning is good.

Venn Diagram—Formalized by John Venn in 1880, it is a visual aid that shows the possible logical relationships between a limited collection of sets

Check Your Understanding

What is formal logic?

What is deductive reasoning and what is meant by "necessarily true"?

What is the difference between and argument and a proposition?

Explain what "subjective truth" is.

Explain social/consensual theories of truth.

Explain the social constructivist perspective on truth.

Explain verificationist theories of truth.

Explain coherence theories of truth.

Explain correspondence theory of truth and semantic theory.

What is the role of validity in argumentation?

What is "soundness" of an argument mean?

Name and define the 3 parts of a syllogism
1.

2.

3.

What is a categorical syllogism?

What is a disjunctive syllogism?

What is a hypothetical syllogism?

What is the difference between an enthymeme and a syllogism?

What are Venn diagrams and how are they useful for argumentation/debate?

What are the three steps used to evaluate a syllogism with a Venn diagram?
1.

2.

3.

Name and define the six types of deductive fallacies then provide an example of each that is not provided to you in the book.

1.

Example:

2.

Example:

3.

Example:

4.

Example:

5.

Example:

6.

Example:

Self-Assessment: Basic concepts - facts, propositions, truth, and argument

1. Which of the following are propositions? If a proposition, what is the subject and what is the predicate? If a proposition, do you think it is true or false?

   a. Sacramento is the capital of Vermont.

   b. $2 + 3 = 7$.

   c. Open the door, please.

   d. $5 + 7 > 10$.

   e. The moon is a satellite of Earth.

   f. $X + 5 = 7$.

   g. Is Hillary Clinton the President of the United States?

   h. This sentence is false.

2. Which of the following are arguments? If an argument, identify its conclusion and the premises. If an argument, do you think it is valid? Is it sound?

   a. Cleveland is the capital of Ohio. All Capitals are fun cities. Cleveland is a fun city.

   b. Bill is putrid. Andy stinks. James is rancid. Boys are smelly.

   c. The solar system was formed over 6 billion years ago.

   d. You can't drive without gas. You've got no gas. You can't drive.

   e. All Huns are mortal and Kublai is a Hun but Kublai is not mortal.

   f. Socrates was the student of Plato so we know he was smart.

   g. If kangaroos had no tails, they'd fall over; roo tails are counterweights.

3. True or false: an argument can be valid but not sound. Explain.

   _____

   _____

   _____

3. Match the theory of truth to the description.
   - _____ Coherentist Theory of Truth
   - _____ Consensual Theory of Truth
   - _____ Verificationist Theory of Truth
   - _____ Semantic Theory of Truth
   - _____ Constructivist Theory of Truth

   A. "P" is true iff P.
   B. It's true if it fits into your cognitive network
   C. P is true if we have made reality that way.
   D. It's true if we all agree it's true.
   E. It's true if you can prove it.

Self-Assessment: Syllogisms

1. Which of the following are syllogisms? If it's a syllogism, is it categorical, disjunctive, or hypothetical? If it's a syllogism, is it valid and/or sound?

   a. All things, which burn, are made of wood. Witches burn. Witches are made of wood.

   b. New York has strict educational standards and low graduation rates. Massachusetts has high educational standards and low rates of graduation. Pennsylvania too. High educational standards result in low graduation rates.

   c. If the cat is fed, it will be happy. When cats are happy they purr. If you feed the cat it will purr.

   d. No Frenchmen make any sense. Jacques is Italian. Sacre Bleu!

   e. Either we live in Bakersfield or we are sad but not both. We are sad. We don't live in Bakersfield.

   f. No zer are huk. Jojo is a zer. Jojo not huk.

2. For the following sets of statements, arrange them to form a valid syllogism. For each, identify the major premise, the minor premise, and the conclusion. For each, identify the minor term, the major term, and the middle term.

   a. Limmy be skinny. When jiggy then skinny. Limmy jiggy.

   b. Jimmy did it. Billy didn't do it. Either Jimmy or Billy did it.

   c. Every bird flies. Tweety flies. Tweety is a bird.

   d. Tonight we dine in London or Paris but not both. Let's take our supper in London. We shall not eat in Paris this evening.

   e. We should attack Naritia. Naritia is a hostile nation developing nuclear weapons. If a hostile nation is developing nuclear weapons, then we should attack it.

3. Assume the following examples are attempts at valid syllogisms. How did they go wrong? Fix each example to make it a valid syllogism.

   a. Witches float. Ducks float. Obviously, ducks and witches weigh the same.

   b. All fish live underwater. Mackerel are fish. Therefore, trout live in trees.

   c. If ketchup is a vegetable then pirates are invisible teleporting ninja monkeys. Ketchup is not a vegetable. Pirates are not invisible teleporting ninja monkeys.

   d. Either sex sells or money talks. Losers don't win. So sex sells.

   e. All copper wires conduct electricity. This is a strand of copper wire. This strand doesn't conduct electricity.

   f. Either it is Tuesday or it is your turn to do the laundry. It isn't Tuesday. Clearly, you don't love me any more.

Self-Assessment: Fixing enthymemes

Supply the missing part of the following enthymemes to form a valid syllogism.

1. He's happy; he's smiling all the time.

2. Naritia has a nuclear bomb. Naritia's neighbors are at risk of nuclear attack.

3. Because most of the sentences are short, the manual will be easy to understand.

4. You didn't speak up in my defense at the meeting. You must be against me too.

5. Her actions, even though legal, must be condemned since they incited violence.

6. Anyone guilty of murder should be executed. Fry him.

7. He cancelled the date because he had too much schoolwork! You've been dumped!

8. Aristotle's *Rhetoric* shouldn't be assigned in this class. It's boring.

9. The use of freon must be outlawed. Freon produces hydrofluorocarbons.

10. Jones is a citizen. He was born in the U.S.

Self-Assessment: Venn Diagrams

1. Identify the basic relationship depicted in the following Venn diagrams:

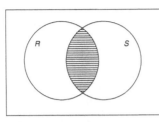

a. _____

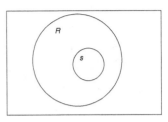

b. _____

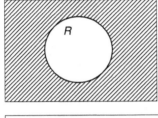

c. _____

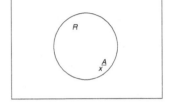

d. _____

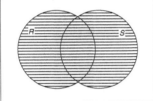

e. _____

2. What syllogism is depicted in the following Venn diagram?

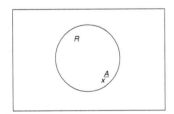

R: reckless   **S:** skatepunks   **A:** Archibald

Major Premise: _____

Minor Premise: _____

Conclusion: _____

3. What syllogism is depicted in the following Venn diagram?

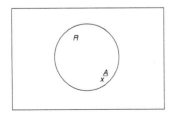

R: red   **S:** sparrow   **A:** Amy

Major Premise: _____

Minor Premise: _____

Conclusion: _____

CHAPTER

6   The Inductive Model

Chapter Objectives

The previous chapter discussed deduction, one of the classical models of effective reasoning. This chapter discusses another model of reasoning: induction. Inductive reasoning is commonly misunderstood to involve reasoning that moves from the specific to the general, in opposition to the tendency of deductive reasoning to move from the general to the specific. While inductive reasoning does begin with particular instances, it may move to the broad or, in the case of analogy, inductive reasoning can move from the specific to other specific instances. It is a mistake to assume that all methods of induction lead to generalizations.

This chapter explores the inductive model of reasoning. First, the chapter distinguishes inductive reasoning from deductive reasoning. Then, the three basic types of inductive arguments, generalization, analogy and causality, are presented. Generalization, the most common form of inductive reasoning, moves from the specific to the general, yet both analogy and causality move from the specific to other specific instances. Tools to evaluate these inductive arguments, such as the test of similarity and difference in metaphor and the use of counterfactuals to evaluate causality, help to illustrate how to evaluate the claims made through induction. The chapter concludes with a discussion of common inductive fallacies.

Logic Meets Reality

Defining Inductive Reasoning

Inductive reasoning involves premises that support the truth of the conclusion, but do not make it entirely certain. The three types of inductive reasoning we will discuss are generalization, analogy, and causality.

Inductive reasoning is distinguished from deductive reasoning, the other classical form, in two ways. First, inductive reasoning does not offer certain conclusions. As noted in the previous chapter, deductive arguments lead to conclusions that are certain. More specifically, if the premises of a deductive argument are true and the deductive argument is valid, then its conclusion is certainly true. Moreover, the conclusion of a valid deductive argument with true premises is not only certain, but necessary: it must be so in all possible worlds in which the premises obtain. Inductive arguments do not offer the same level of certainty. Instead, the conclusions of inductive arguments are never certain, offering only degrees of likelihood.

Understanding this factor as it distinguishes induction and deduction requires an understanding of probability. Probability is the measurement of the likelihood of an event. Probability offers a value between zero and 1, with one being a 100% chance, or certainty, that something will happen. In a valid deductive argument with true premises, the probability of the conclusion is 1. The likelihood that a fair coin, when flipped, will turn up heads is about 50%. Inductive reasoning will never generate conclusions which are 100% likely.

Another way to understand this distinction is that inductive arguments can never be valid. Validity is tested for deductive arguments by assuming the argument's premises true and examining whether the conclusion is necessarily true. Since the conclusions of inductive arguments are never certain, much less necessary, inductive arguments can never be valid. Although important, this distinction does not render inductive reasoning useless: coming to a conclusion which is 99.99% likely true can be very worthwhile, despite not having reached certainty.

Second, inductive reasoning begins from the specific and moves toward a conclusion that may or may not be general. This is sometimes called bottom-up reasoning in contrast to the top-down reasoning style of deductive reasoning. Deductive reasoning begins with the general or universal statements and concludes to either a specific case or instance or other general claims. Deductive reasoning extracts the inferences and implications of general and universal propositions, developing our understanding in a "top-down" fashion. Inductive reasoning starts with specific examples, individual pieces of data, and particular cases. Inductive reasoning may lead the individual to reflect broadly or to draw relationships between the instance of the specific to another specific case. Inductive reasoning puts together the similarities and differences, extracts the variance and the invariants of experiences, and seeks to figure out the linkages between examples, developing our understanding in a "bottom-up" fashion.

Finally, inductive reasoning is the way most of us reason on a daily basis. From the moment of birth, we explore and examine the world and ourselves, seeking to put together the pieces of lived experience. We do not begin with universal truths and general knowledge, both required to perform deductive reasoning, but with the individual sights, sounds, smells, and feelings of perception, the stuff which induction works upon. As we mature, we are taught and discover universal and general truths and learn deductive processes, but every day we continue to rely on inductive processes to make sense of the world. This third contrast between inductive and deductive reasoning notes that deductive reasoning is rarely available and used while inductive reasoning is commonly available and practiced.

Deduction

- [ ] certainty
- [ ] top down
- [ ] rare

Induction

- [ ] probability
- [ ] bottom up
- [ ] common

The Scientific Method

The **Scientific Method** is a series of steps used by researchers to acquire, test and revise knowledge. Science requires its method of inquiry to involve measureable phenomena and to be based upon empirics. The Scientific Method combines elements of deductive and inductive reasoning to gather and interpret information about the world. While steps are sometimes combined or omitted, the Scientific Method is generally composed of four steps.

First, we observe that our perceptions and experiences indicate unresolved matters, perhaps even incongruities, and pose questions. This first step, noticing that we do not understand something about ourselves or the world is the motive and initiator of the scientific method, but the decision to address those mysteries in a scientific manner is also a part of this first step.

Second, we posit hypotheses, construct explanations, or design models to make sense of what we have come to experience. Hypotheses are testable individual statements that attempt to make sense of our experiences, while explanations attempt to make sense of entire groups of experiences, and models look to understand the interactions of large groups of observed phenonomen.

Third, the hypotheses, explanations, and models are tested by gathering further experiences and observations, sometimes by conducting experiments. Solid hypotheses, explanations, and models will pass the tests used to evaluate them for a time. The scientific method does not halt in these situations, but continues to test our understanding again and again. Eventually, even the best of the hypotheses, explanations, and models will begin to fail the tests thrown at them as observations inconsistent with them begin to accumulate.

Fourthly, when our hypotheses, explanations, and models fail the tests used to evaluate them, we return to the second step and posit new hypotheses, formulate new explanations, and construct new models. Those new tentative understandings are then tested and the process repeats without end, or until our understanding of a domain of knowledge is perfected. Whether this end state, a complete understanding of an area of human experience has or can ever be achieved, is an open question.

Finally, communication is an indispensable part of the Scientific Method, even though it is not one of the steps of the process. We should communicate to other thinkers and researchers each step of the process. Communication within the scientific method is critical because scientists and researchers work both individually and collectively. Each builds upon the work of others. Scientists will often also attempt to replicate the experiments conducted by other researchers in order to see if they gather the same results.

During the completion of these steps, we use both deductive and inductive reasoning. Induction is used in the initial making of observations and in the gathering of the data during the experiment. Deduction occurs during the drawing out of the implications of the experiment. Deduction ultimately uses the information gathered through induction to draw conclusions. These two methods of reasoning are complementary and both are necessarily used by scientists when conducting research.

One of those cool looping table thingies showing circularity of science

Generalization

Generalization takes the form of identifying multiple examples and then coming to a general conclusion based upon those examples. Generalization is the most common form of inductive reasoning. In fact, generalization is so common that it causes many to believe that generalization is the only type of inductive reasoning.

Since the conclusion of an inductive argument is never perfectly certain, generalizations can yield both true and false conclusions. For example, a student may observe multiple dogs. Each dog studied has two eyes. The student concludes through generalization that all dogs have two eyes. Another student may interview people at the mall. The interview asks every person where they live. All of the people interviewed live in Bakersfield. The student generalizes to conclude that every person at the mall lives in Bakersfield.

Effective generalization requires knowledge of statistics. Statistics will guide the researcher to develop a representative sample size. Statistics will also help to determine if the members of the sample are representative of the greater population, which impacts whether the results collected are similarly applicable.

Categorization is a simple method of induction closely associated with generalization. Children often use categories to support their inductive reasoning. For example, a child may be able to look at a group of vehicles and recognize that the Ford, Toyota and Cadillac are all cars. That same child can then recognize that the helicopter is not a car even though it is a vehicle. Similarly, children can use categories to distinguish between different types of cats and different types of dogs. These children may not know particular breeds but they will be able to identify what is a dog and what is a cat based upon personal knowledge of other dogs and cats.

Analogy

The second method of induction is **Analogy**. Analogies draw a conclusion from one case or example to another case or example. Analogies have been popularly used on standardized tests to evaluate the critical thinking skills of the test taker.

For example, if your best friend saw a movie that just came out, and was bored by it, you might conclude that you would also be bored by it. In a policy context, if one state tried a fiscal strategy which revived their stagnant economy, it might be reasonable to conclude that another state should attempt the same fiscal strategy to revive its own economic performance. These examples notice something about one case and conclude to another, similar, case.

Analogy is different from generalization in two significant ways. First, analogy uses only one or two examples at most. On the other hand, generalization looks at many examples before forming a conclusion. The second difference is the form of the conclusion offered by the analogy. A generalization offers a generalized, or broad, conclusion. In contrast, the conclusion of an analogy is always a specific example or case, rather than a broad general conclusion.

As a method of logical reasoning, analogy has some important drawbacks. First, analogy has no validity. In addition, it is problematic. Whether or not there are similarities or differences between any two things that are being compared does not rest on the features of those things. It rests on the quality of the arguer, or the debater that is trying to take apart the analogy. Ultimately, the strength of an analogy depends considerably upon the strength of the debater advancing it as an argument.

The basic way to evaluate the strength of an analogy is to evaluate the similarities and differences between the cases being discussed. If the similarities are more important or greater in extent, then it is a good analogy. If the differences are not, then it is a bad analogy.

Similarity & Difference

The basic test of the utility of an analogy is the comparison of similarities and differences. If the similarities are greater than the differences, then the analogy may be considered a good one. However, if the differences are greater than the similarities, the analogy may not be useful or appropriate.

The determination of similarity and difference is inherently fallible due to the position of the evaluator. Position impacts the availability to observe. Position also influences contextual relevance. One individual's position and resultant perception can lead to the identification of similarities between two objects, whereas another individual may focus instead upon the identification of differences even when evaluating the same two objects.

Differential levels of knowledge will further impact the evaluation of similarities and differences. For example, an individual unaware of the fact that a dolphin is a mammal may point to the similarities of a dolphin and a shark to determine that a dolphin is a fish. However, an individual aware of the characters of a mammal will see important factors distinguishing the difference between the dolphin and the shark, such as the fact that the dolphin is warm-blooded and births live young.

Metaphor

A **metaphor** is a specialized type of analogy that compares two unrelated objects in order to point to a shared characteristic or sameness. The metaphor asserts that the two are alike in that one point. A metaphor is composed of two parts. The first part, the **tenor**, is the subject to which the metaphor ascribes characteristics. The second part of the metaphor is the vehicle. The **vehicle** is the subject whose characteristic is borrowed in order to describe the tenor.

Students are often introduced to metaphors within the context of studying literature. Authors will use metaphors to forcibly present an idea. Specialized types of metaphors found within literature include puns, parables and allegories.

William Shakespeare offered one of the most famous examples of a metaphor:

All the world's a stage,
And all the men and women merely players;
They have their exits and their entrances (As You Like It, Act II, Scene VII).

The first line states the conclusion of the metaphor and the premises are offered in the second and third line. Within this metaphor, the tenor is the world. The vehicle is the stage. The world shares the characteristic of having players fulfill their roles, complete with entrances and exits, with a stage.

Metaphors can be distinguished from other types of analogies found within literature. In particular, a metaphor is often contrasted with a simile. A similar argues that two things are alike, often using the language "like" or "as" to connect the two. In contrast, the wording of a metaphor is much more forceful. The metaphor does not say that the two things are alike; it asserts that one thing is another.

Causality

The Basics

Causality, the third type of inductive reasoning, contends that one thing produces, creates or causes another. Structurally, a causality argument contains the identification of a cause and an effect. The **antecedent** is the cause. The **consequent** is the effect. Causality is also known as causal induction. Understanding causality is critical for human beings and essential for our individual and collective survival.

Counterfactuals

Counterfactuals serve as the test for evaluating a causal claim. A **counterfactual** is a counter to a fact claim. As with the other forms of inductive reasoning, causality is problematic. The argument is highly dependent upon the ability of the arguer to offer it persuasively.

Counterfactual analysis involves a consideration of the nearest possible world to the one in which the antecedent obtains. The evaluation of the causality claim using counterfactual analysis requires the completion of three steps. First, this evaluation involves leaving our reality and going to another possible world containing the things that could be. Everything is the same within this possible world as the real world, with the exception of the one antecedent being evaluated. Second, the fictional world is then studied in order to determine if the consequence is the result. Finally, the evaluation of the causality argument can be conducted using the information collected from the counterfactual world. If the decision is that the consequence obtained in that possible world is true, then the counter factual is true in our world. On the other hand, if it's not true, than it would be concluded to be false.

For example, a student spends the night partying and drives to class while still intoxicated. The morning is very foggy. The student gets into the car accident. What caused the accident? Many would argue that the driver being intoxicated caused the accident.

However, causality is tested by considering the removal of the purported cause in order to determine what would happen. If the student wasn't drunk, would the accident have still happened? This question is difficult to answer. Fog can obscure vision and fog has contributed to car accidents in the past, so it is possible that the accident would have happened even if the student had not been tired and drunk. This acknowledgment undermines the idea of the student's state being the cause of the accident.

Inductive Fallacies

Not all inductive reasoning is valid. **Inductive fallacies** are those arguments which move from the specific to the general or the specific in an erroneous manner which ultimately leads to an inaccurate conclusion. This section provides a brief discussion of the inductive fallacies you are most likely to observe: cherry picking, confirmation bias, bandwagon, hasty generalization, slippery slope, false cause, and weak analogy.

Cherry Picking

To begin, **cherry picking** occurs when an individual points to a limited number of cases in order to support a particular conclusion, while also ignoring those cases which disprove the conclusion. Cherry picking may be intentional or accidental. Cherry picking is also known as the fallacy of incomplete evidence.

Cherry picking is a practice found within a wide range of real-life settings. As with many other forms of inductive reasoning, cherry picking is problematic and the extent of its problematic nature is dependent upon the actions of the arguer. For example, modern resume writing commonly employs cherry picking. In fact, this is an innocuous and even necessary practice. Employers do not want to know everything about the life of the candidate. So, the job applicant commonly cherry picks the most relevant and typically most positive things to share to the interviewer. However, most interviewers recognize resumes as one sided and will ask questions in order to gather more information about a candidate.

For example, a resume may provide an individual's degree and place of education. However, the resume will exclude the fact that the applicant was recently fired for being intoxicated in the workplace. A resume will also only highlight personal strengths and ignore weaknesses. Cherry picking ultimately suppresses some of the truth in order to emphasize some of the truth that the arguer views as important to furthering the argument. The applicant will list good qualities and ignore bad qualities when writing a resume because the applicant wants to get the job.

Confirmation Bias

Confirmation bias is a form of cherry picking which describes how individuals will tend to focus upon data that supports their pre-existing beliefs. Confirmation bias also leads individuals to interpret ambiguous results as confirming their existing beliefs, rather than acknowledging the ambiguity. Confirmation bias further means that individuals ignore research, data and information that does not conform to their beliefs.

Confirmation bias is an especially common practice used to protect beliefs regarding deeply entrenched, emotional or otherwise difficult views. Writers face a high risk of confirmation bias when preparing a written work. For example, a student preparing a paper on a controversial subject may spend all of her time collecting research that agrees with her views. She may then overlook or ignore those studies which disagree with her and the thesis of her paper. Similarly, a reporter investigating a court case may only interview witnesses and experts who agree with the reporter's legal assessment. In both cases, the result will be a written project influenced by the author's bias.

Bandwagon

Out of all the fallacies, the bandwagon fallacy causes the most irritation, and yet, can be highly successful on unsuspecting audiences. You will want to avoid this fallacy and all fallacies during your argumentation process because it reflects poorly on your credibility, calls your ethics into consideration, and just looks bad. Now, the bandwagon fallacy is simple, it asserts that because everyone else is doing it so should you. The bandwagon fallacy appeals to your sense of conformity, your desire to be similar, and the idea that we should be "keeping up." You will have seen this fallacy in action when your child comes to you begging for an iPad because, "everyone else in my class has iPad!" There are actually a few types of bandwagon fallacies, but they all basically argue the same way, which is by purposely constructing an argument that appeals the audience's desire to fit in or been seen as "normal."

Appeal to common belief bandwagon fallacy: "You need to understand and come to see what 7 out of 10 American's already do, that legalizing marijuana is a good thing."

Appeal to common practice bandwagon fallacy: "You should buy your elementary age child a cell-phone, most kids these days have cell phones and data plans."

Hasty Generalization

This is probably the most used fallacy in interpersonal, small group, and college argumentation classes. The **hasty generalization** fallacy is just as it sounds, it is a generalization that an arguer makes hastily (with little consideration). In direct terms, hasty generalizations are inferences drawn from insufficient data.

"A friend of mine signed up through the new health exchange web site, no problem. They are working great!"

"My uncle began smoking at age 15, smoked five packs a day and lived until he was 83 years old. As a result, smoking isn't unhealthy like they say."

Slippery Slope

The next most common fallacy is called the "slippery slope." The **slippery slope** fallacy you have seen from the time you were small. You might have seen it in your local anti-drug campaigns, during parental reasoning, or while discussing politics. The slippery slope argument is basically what it sounds like, it asserts that if you take one tiny step in a certain direction you will fall head first in a downward tumble and that you will not be able to stop that momentum until you have hit the bottom of the hill.

The "fear tactic" is often used in conjunction with the slippery slope fallacy. Frequently, arguers will assert that one small choice will just domino into a catastrophe and that catastrophe will be something to greatly fear or avoid. The key to not committing this fallacy is to make sure you have enough evidence to support the claim that If A, then B, if B then C, and if C then D, and that nothing will be able to stop that result. In short, the key to having a consequence argument not be a slippery slope fallacy is to ensure your data supports the claim totally.

> *"If they pass this waiting period on guns, they will do restrictions on assault rifles, and that will lead to gun bans everywhere. Stop the gun-grabbers now!"*

> *"If you allow your child to watch a cartoon like Tom and Jerry, they will get hooked on violent video games, and then will do who knows what!"*

False Cause or "Post hoc, ergo propter hoc"

In Latin, the false cause fallacy means, "after this, therefore because of this." Although that may sound confusing it is actually quite simple. What **false cause** fallacy means is that false cause fallacy occurs when an arguers asserts that because one event followed another even the first event cause the second event. You can see why this is weak. Of course, there are occasions where one thing did cause another to occur right after, but more often, the cause of a given effect is not always due to what ever happened just before it.

This is a dangerous fallacy because it can be convincing to an audience who can see and understand the relationship between the two events, but has not really thought it through. Causality is difficult to demonstrate and control, so most often it is difficult to prove a cause and much easier to prove a correlation.

Slippery Slope - an inductive fallacy that inappropriately assigns causation for major events to a relatively minor event

- Confirmation Bias - a form of cherry picking which describes how individuals will tend to focus upon data that supports their pre-existing beliefs.

False cause - this fallacy occurs when an arguer asserts that because one event followed another even the first event cause the second event

- cherry picking - occurs when an individual points to a limited number of cases in order to support a particular conclusion, while also ignoring those cases which disprove the conclusion.

Hasty generalization - are inferences drawn from insufficient data.

"Every time we won a game I wore one blue sock and one red sock. Therefore, if we want to keep winning I need to keep wearing my socks."

"Becky lost 14lbs in one month. She started eating those yogurt-covered pretzels twice a week this month. Therefore yogurt covered pretzels made Becky loose weight."

"Ice cream sales increase every June. The number of common colds lowers substantially every July. Therefore: higher ice cream consumption cures the common cold."

False Analogy also known as "Weak Analogy"

Analogies, as you have learned, are excellent forms of argumentation at times, but like any other argument they run the risk of becoming fallacious. The way to keep yourself from creating a false analogy is to be critical of your analogy. Make sure the things you are comparing are only different in very irrelevant ways.

An analogy-based argument presents the following idea:

X and Y are similar.
Since X has property A, Y has property A

You know the analogy is fallacious if when you critique the analogy you find that there is a difference between the two that ultimately affects whether they both have property A.

"Education is like business, just as business is primarily concerned with the overall profit, so should education."

Conclusion

In contrast to deductive reasoning (as presented in the previous chapter), inductive reasoning does not offer an irrefutable conclusion. Deductive arguments lead to conclusions that are certain. If logically sound and valid, the deductive argument's conclusion must be so. Inductive arguments do not offer the same level of certainty. Instead, they offer conclusions that are likely to be so.

Inductive reasoning is often informally described as the logical move from the specific to the general. However, this characterization is mistaken. Inductive reasoning does include reasoning that moves from the specific to the general, such as in generalizations, but inductive reasoning also includes analogies, which move from one specific to another specific. Inductive reasoning is defined not by a general conclusion but by the initial basis upon the specific. Inductive reasoning does not argue from general statements. It argues based upon individual instances. Both inductive and deductive reasoning are used by researchers within the Scientific Method.

The three types of inductive argument are generalization, analogy and causality. Generalization, the most common form of inductive reasoning, leads to a generalized conclusion by evaluating specific cases. Analogy leads to another example or instance. The value of an analogy is tested by evaluating the similarities and differences of the things being compared. Causality argues from the antecedent, or cause, to the consequent, or effect. All of these examples of inductive reasoning begin their arguments with specifics, rather than generalizations.

Inductive fallacies move from the general to produce an inaccurate conclusion. They are also known as faulty generalizations. Common inductive fallacies are cherry picking, hasty generalization, false analogy, confirmation bias and the slippery slope.

Key Terms

Analogy—A type of inductive reasoning that looks at one or two examples to determine a conclusion about another case or example

Antecedent—The component of a causality argument that is responsible for causing the observed effect upon the consequent

Consequent—The effect generated by the antecedent within a causality claim

Causality—The type of inductive reasoning that contends that one thing produces/creates/causes another

Cherry Picking—A type of inductive fallacy that focuses solely upon a limited number of cases to prove a point, while ignoring the larger number of cases that contradict that point. Synonymous with the *fallacy of incomplete evidence.*

Confirmation Bias—A form of cherry picking which describes how individuals will tend to focus upon data that supports their pre-existing beliefs.

Counterfactual—A counter to a fact claim and a useful tool for evaluating causality arguments

Dicto Simpliciter: Hasty Generalization—drawing a definite conclusion using only a small sample, rather than utilizing statistics that are more descriptive and appropriate for the typical situation. The Fallacy of Composition

False Analogy—A flawed analogy

Faulty Generalizations—Synonym for *inductive fallacies.* An inaccurate argument that moves from the specific to the general.

False cause—this fallacy occurs when an arguer asserts that because one event followed another even the first event cause the second event

Generalization—The most common form of inductive reasoning, generalization takes the form of identifying multiple examples and then coming to a general conclusion based upon those examples

Inductive Fallacies—Arguments which move from the specific to the general in an erroneous manner. Also known as *faulty generalizations.*

Inductive Reasoning—Reasoning that involves premises that support the truth of the conclusion, but do not make it entirely certain.

Metaphor—A specialized type of analogy that compares two unrelated objects in order to point to a shared characteristic or sameness

Post hoc ergo propter hoc—An inductive fallacy, After the fact therefore because of the fact

Probability—The field of study which measures the likelihood of an event

The Scientific Method—The specific steps used by scientific researchers to gather, critique and revise new knowledge

Slippery Slope—An inductive fallacy that inappropriately assigns causation for major events to a relatively minor event

Tenor—In a metaphor, the subject of the metaphor's conclusion

Vehicle—In a metaphor, the subject whose characteristic is borrowed in order to describe the tenor.

Name: _____   **Class:** _____

Check Your Understanding

What is inductive reasoning?

What is the difference between deductive and inductive reasoning?

What is the scientific method? Explain each step in detail.

1.

2.

3.

4.

What make an effective generalization?

What makes an effective analogy?

What is the difference between an analogy and a generalization?

What exactly is a metaphor? Define it, provide and example, and detail the two parts that compose it.

What is causality and what does it contain?

What is a counterfactual and what does it involve?

Define and exemplify what "cherry picking" is.

Define and exemplify what "confirmation bias" is.

Define and exemplify what the bandwagon fallacy is. Provide an example that was not given in the book.

What is a "hasty generalization"? Provide an example that was not given in the book.

What does it mean when some commits a "slippery slope" fallacy? Provide an example that was not given in the book.

"False cause" is also known as "post hoc, ergo propter hoc"- please explain this fallacy. Provide an example that was not given in the book.

A false analogy is also known as a weak analogy- please explain this fallacy. Provide an example that was not given in the book.

Self-Assessment: Inductive arguments

1. Which type of inductive arguments are the following?

    a. Cigarette smoking results in lung cancer. Those who smoke often develop lung cancer.

    b. We surveyed 1,000 college students and the vast majority use social media. College students are into that stuff.

    c. Raising the drinking age in Minnesota substantially lowered drunk driving deaths. Raising the drinking age in California will do the same thing.

    d. Every Republican I have met wears nice shoes. Republicans spend lots of money on footwear.

    e. His Salmon Carpaccio was delicious. His Lobster Newberg will be amazing!

2. Inductive arguments never get to certain conclusions. Give an example of where the difference between being 95% sure and being 100% sure might matter.

    _____

    _____

    _____

    _____

3. Can you give an example of when you used an analogy recently?

    _____

    _____

    _____

    _____

4. Please evaluate the following counterfactual claim: "If your parents had never met, you wouldn't have been born." Is it true? How did you come to that conclusion?

    _____

    _____

    _____

    _____

CHAPTER

7 Foundations of Debate

Chapter Objectives

Debate has a storied history in American higher education. As many as 500 American colleges and universities currently have competitive intercollegiate debate programs supported by at least one faculty member serving as the director of debate. Many debate programs enjoy substantial endowments and the ability to hire additional coaches or fund graduate students to serve as coaching assistants. These programs have anywhere from two to over a hundred students actively traveling to compete at debate tournaments across the nation. It is a conservative estimate that millions of dollars and hundreds of thousands of hours annually are given to competitive intercollegiate debate in the United States. Debate is also very popular within high schools. In fact, many successful high school debaters earn scholarships that will enable them to debate while attending college.

This chapter provides a firm foundation for the discussion of debate. Upon completing this chapter, you will:

- Understand debate as rhetoric and argument in action
- Learn the role of topics in determining the affirmative's burden of proof and the negative's burden of rejoinder
- Gain familiarity with the different associations responsible for organizing competitive debate

The background information found within this chapter will help you to prepare to participate in debate.

Debate as Rhetoric and Argument in Action

Contemporary debate is rhetoric and argument in action. As noted in previous chapters, **rhetoric** is persuasion. **Persuasion** is the act of attempting to influence an individual's or group's attitudes, behaviors, beliefs, intentions, or motivations. Rhetoric may focus upon topics both personal and professional. It may be offered in a private setting or publicly. Rhetoric dates back to the world's oldest book: *The Maxims of Ptah-Hotep*.

Argument is a set of statements, one of which serves as a conclusion, while the others together provide support for that conclusion. A working understanding of argumentation rests on a foundation of a few basic concepts. These concepts, each problematic in its own way, underlie argument and, thus, philosophy. The integration of these terms into one's working vocabulary provides the basis for understanding both argumentation and debate.

An argument is a set of propositions. **Propositions** are defined as statements that are true or false. Truth is a property of propositions or statements. One says of a proposition or statement that it is TRUE if it is the case. One says of a proposition or statement that it is FALSE if it is not the case. One proposition is the conclusion and the other propositions support the conclusion.

A debate is a structured deliberation in which opponents argue opposing viewpoints. It is the application and combination of rhetoric and argumentation. While debate incorporates methods of persuasion, it encompasses far more than rhetoric. Debate is contention and discussion, disputation and controversy. It may include deductive reasoning or factual argumentation, and often incorporates both.

Debate is a common and critical component of human life. Debate is found throughout a nation's political bodies. Politicians, analysts, and civilians engage in debate when they propose, consider, evaluate, and oppose resolutions, bills, and regulations. These public debates are often decided by a vote that occurs at the end of the deliberation period.

Debate is also an important part of education. Many schools house and support debate programs. These recreational programs enable students to research and argue resolutions for recreational and educational purposes. Numerous justifications are offered regarding the educational value of such expenditures. The classic rationale is that participation in debate teaches students critical thinking skills.

The link between debating and critical thinking might not be immediately obvious. However, this relationship is both time-tested and robust. Engagement in the activity of debate enables students to participate in an activity developed specifically to encourage the application of argumentation knowledge and the growth of critical thinking ability. Because of the importance of critical thinking abilities to our common future, debate educators have looked to justify debate programs via the salutary effect of participation in competitive intercollegiate debate upon critical thinking skills. The debate community nearly uniformly believes that participation in competitive intercollegiate debate increases critical thinking abilities, and there are many prima facia reasons to believe that debate participation does increase critical thinking ability: students are expected to construct understandings of multiple subject domains by researching complex issues, to synthesize diverse information into coherent positions, to formulate arguments from conflicting viewpoints, and finally to advocate their arguments in a competitive atmosphere. Debate, offered at high schools, colleges, and universities around the world, has proven to improve the critical thinking of participants in as short a period of time as one semester. Through pre-round preparation for a debate, the student learns how to apply critical thinking to real-world problems through the research and development of potential solutions. During the actual debate round, students learn how to think quickly and respond to arguments under the stress of competition. Participation in debate also introduces students to a community of critical thinkers that includes educators, philosophers, lawyers, scientists, and debate coaches.

Debate is often associated with advocacy. Students passionate about a particular goal or critical perspective find their voice within a debate round. However, a debate position is not always synonymous with personal support. In fact, facility and experience with debate should enable the individual to engage in argumentation on either side of an argument. The switch-side nature of the activity forces students out of their comfort zone, encouraging personal inquiry and critical thought.

Resolutions/Claims at Issue and Types of Claims

The **resolution** is a normative statement that outlines the general subject of the debate. The resolution states one way for a particular group or entity to act within a particular context. Debate resolutions are crafted regularly by debate associations, resulting in a range of topics that will be debated by students who compete for multiple years.

Resolutions advance the claim at issue. The **claim** is the conclusion of the argument advanced by a debater. It is the thesis of the argument. Sometimes, the claim is the resolution itself. The affirmative may seek to defend the entire statement of the resolution and the negative would then focus upon undermining the resolution. More commonly, however, the affirmative will select an example of the resolution to defend.

Once a claim is established, the debater must build the claim by establishing grounds, warrants, and backing. **Grounds** is the reasoning used to support the claim. Sound grounds will show that the claim is similarly solid. Weak grounds will suggest that the claim is not strong and therefore vulnerable to attack.

Warrants bridge the space between the grounds and the claim. A **warrant** is the reason why the provided ground supports the advanced claim. A warrant may take the form of evidence or it may take the form of reasoning. **Backing** is the evidence used to support a warrant.

Debaters will often use the phrase "claim without a warrant." This statement, when leveled as an argument against an opponent, suggests that the claim being made by the debater lacks sufficient evidence to justify its support. The idea of a claim without a warrant is not limited to a debate round, however. In many cases, individuals will casually make recommendations without supporting that recommendation with evidence.

For example, one individual may tell another, "In the upcoming presidential election, you should vote for this candidate." This statement is a claim without a warrant. The speaker has not identified a reason to vote for the candidate. The argument to vote for the particular candidate would be strengthened with evidence or reasons. The speaker could identify the candidate's voting record on certain issues as a reason for the vote. The speaker could also identify the party of the candidate and party loyalty as a reason for the vote. The speaker might also argue that the identified candidate is a better choice than the opposition. Any of these reasons would qualify as warrants. They would strengthen the claim being advanced by providing reasons why the recommended action would be a good idea and should be undertaken by the listener.

The resolution is a claim. It states the conclusion of the argument. The debate then is about the warrants supporting that claim.

Resolutions vary. Two types of resolutions are most common within competitive debate. The first type is a policy resolution. A **policy resolution** identifies a policy action that should be undertaken. The policy resolution will tend to contain two parts: the agent of action and the action. The agent of action is the subject of the sentence and identifies the entity that will undertake the action. The following examples offer a series of actual policy resolutions used recently by debate organizations.

Sample Policy Resolutions

2012–2013 National Policy Debate High School Resolution:

> The United States federal government should substantially increase its transportation infrastructure investment in the United States

2011–2012 CEDA-NDT Intercollegiate Policy Resolution:

> Resolved: The United States Federal Government should substantially increase its democracy assistance for one or more of the following: Bahrain, Egypt, Libya, Syria, Tunisia, Yemen.

As these examples illustrate, a policy resolution often identifies the U.S. federal government, or a subset or agency of the government, as the actor. The qualifier "should" illustrates the normative and debatable nature of the resolution. In each of these resolutions, the debate will revolve around whether the U.S. federal government should undertake a particular action.

In contrast to a policy resolution, a **values resolution** will offer a statement of a value that ought to be advocated. The values resolution differs from a policy resolution in two substantial ways. First, the values resolution may, but does not always, contain an agent of action. Second, a values resolution may, but only rarely recommends an action to be undertaken. As an alternative, the values resolution may identify an idea or concept as good or just without encouraging action. The following are samples of real values resolutions used in competitive debate.

Sample Values Resolutions

March/April 2012 High School Lincoln-Douglas Resolution:

Targeted killing is a morally permissible foreign policy tool.

2009 NFL Nationals:

Resolved: Military conscription is unjust.

The format of the values debate differs from a policy debate in the status of the actor. The resolution need not identify the specific actor since the resolution is about committing to a value rather than taking a posited action. The debaters and the judges serve as the actors who must determine whether they will agree or disagree with the value raised by the resolution.

By default, both policy resolutions and values resolutions tend to advocate action, behavior, or belief that is different from the status quo. The **status quo** is the present or existing status of things. This resolutional wording then permits the side not supporting the resolution to strategically advocate the status quo as superior. The next section discusses in greater detail the responsibilities of debaters arguing on either side of the resolution.

The Burden of Proof and the Burden of Rejoinder

The resolution divides the debate into two sides: the affirmative and the negative. Debate is a switch-sides activity. This means that debaters will be organized to argue both sides of the resolution. In one round, a debater will affirm the resolution as true but in another round, the same debater will be required to argue against the resolution or argue against the debater who is affirming the resolution as true.

The **affirmative** is responsible for supporting the resolution as true. The affirmative side is often referenced as the Aff. The affirmative may argue that the resolution, as a whole, is true. This whole resolution strategy is particularly common in values debate, where the resolution is a simple and clear statement that can be discussed in the relatively short amount of time within a debate round.

However, as the examples within the previous section illustrate, policy resolutions are often very broad, encompassing a wide range of potential activities. In the real world, policies with such broad language are rarely adopted. Instead, policymakers will look at a problem and propose solutions that fall within the general scope of the resolution. Policy debaters engage in a similar process. The affirmative within a policy debate will often choose to **parametricize**. Within this strategy, the affirmative will choose to defend an example of the resolution as true. This example is typically presented as a plan and is common within policy debate.

The affirmative and negative have different burdens that they are expected to fulfill during the course of the debate. To begin, the affirmative has the burden of proof. **The burden of proof** is an obligation to overcome any presumption against the truth of the resolution. This obligation is fulfilled by offering warrants and backing that detail solid reasons to support the resolution.

In contrast, the **negative** has the burden of rejoinder. Once the affirmative team meets the burden of proof, the negative expected to respond to the affirmative's claims. Through the **burden of rejoinder**, the negative side essentially agrees that the resolution or subset of the resolution that the affirmative has chosen to defend is the focus of the round. The negative will tend to argue against the affirmative's claims.

The burden of proof is essential to the negative's ability to fulfill the burden of rejoinder because it enables the negative to prepare for the affirmative's arguments. The resolution identifies the general claim that will be debated in the round. An affirmative that does not fulfill its burden of proof may elect to talk about an issue that has nothing to do with the resolution. That strategy undermines the ability of the negative to fulfill its burden of rejoinder because the negative may not have evidence or prepared arguments to discuss the affirmative's additional issues. If the affirmative does not fulfill its burden of proof, the affirmative will likely lose the debate round. Similarly, if the affirmative does fulfill its burden of proof and the negative fails to fulfill its burden of rejoinder, then the negative will likely lose the debate round.

Ultimately, the burden of rejoinder and the burden of proof are at the heart of a good debate because they encourage clash. **Clash** occurs when both sides of the debate are discussing the same arguments and issues. If there is no clash, the debate round will likely not be very intellectually interesting. One side will argue its set of claims, while the other side argues another. For a judge or an audience member, the lack of clash is confusing. It becomes difficult to follow the round because the debaters are talking about different things. It is also uninteresting because instead of extending and expanding upon their arguments with new claims, the two sides merely repeat their arguments over and over again. As a debater, you should be aware of the importance of clash and the need to fulfill your assigned burden according to what side of the resolution you are expected to debate in a given round.

Forms of Competitive Debate

Competitive debate is described by two key features. The first is the number of participants. Debates may feature one person debating another or a team of debaters competing against another team. The second is the type of resolution debated. As the previous section touched upon briefly, a policy resolution will discuss the passage of a particular policy or action, while a values debate will focus upon the intellectual endorsement of an idea or value. Each of these distinctions, and their impact upon a debate's format, will be discussed in greater detail within this section.

The Number of Debate Participants

Some competitive debate formats involve one person debating another, or 1v1. For example, moot court debate in law school often has just two participants who debate each other in front of a judge. Lincoln Douglas debate at the college level is also one person (the affirmative) versus another person (the negative). One versus one debate is discussed in greater detail in chapter nine.

Many competitive debates feature teams composed of two people. Two-person debate is called team debate. Team debate shares many of the features of one on one debate but the addition of two more speakers does create unique structural features and strategic options for the debate round. Team debate is discussed in greater detail in chapter ten.

Resolutional Wording

Competitive debate is often divided into two categories: policy and values debate. Policy debate features a policy resolution that guides debaters to argue about whether an action should be taken. Values debate features a values resolution and involves debaters arguing about the particular intellectual endorsement of an ethical idea.

Different Forms of Debate

At both the high school and college level, debaters have access to a wide range of debate activities. Many of these activities are distinguished by one of the two resolutional considerations already noted. Some debate formats feature teams, while others pit one debater against another. Some debate formats are organized around policy debate, while others prefer values debate. Policy debate is primarily guided by the presence and use of a policy resolution. Some policy debate formats feature one debater against another, while some offer team debate. Values-oriented debate similarly is offered in both team and one versus one format. In addition, these debate activities are distinguished by additional factors, such as research burdens, the value of entertainment, and the timing of speeches. It is worth noting some of the major forms of debate before moving on.

Lincoln-Douglas Debate

Lincoln-Douglas debate is named for the 1858 series of debates between Abraham Lincoln and Stephen Douglas. Lincoln and Douglas debated in a one versus one format and Lincoln-Douglas debate is, not surprisingly, also one on one debate. This type of debate is also known as LD debate.

However, the type of resolution debated by Lincoln-Douglas debaters depends upon grade level. High school Lincoln-Douglas debate involves values debate. At the college level, Lincoln-Douglas debaters argue policy resolutions. The lasting similarity between the LD debate across the different age levels is its involvement of just two competitors.

Policy Debate

Policy debate is debate guided by a policy resolution. The primary content of a policy debate involves the discussion of whether an action, typically undertaken by a government entity, is a good idea. Policy debate is offered at both the high school and the college level. Policy debate includes one versus one format and team formats.

Many different policy debate organizations exist. As already noted, Lincoln-Douglas debate features one debater arguing against another. The National Forensic League also sponsors policy debate for high school participants. At the college level, team policy debate is organized by groups such as the Cross-Examination Debate Association (CEDA) and the National Debate Tournament (NDT).

Parliamentary Debate

Parliamentary debate is a competitive debate format governed by the rules of parliamentary procedure. Parliamentary debate is one of the oldest forms of debate and it is practiced in many countries around the world. Parliamentary debate can feature one versus one debate, but it is more common for parliamentary debate to feature teams of two. Parliamentary debate may use a values resolution or a policy resolution.

Parliamentary debate is distinguished from other debate options by a couple of key features. First, parliamentary debate tends to minimize the use and importance of evidence. Instead, parliamentary debate is judged according to the arguments and wit of the participating debaters. As a result, parliamentary debate tends to feature more humor than other debate formats.

Mock Trial and Moot Court

Competitive judicial debate emulates the procedures conducted within the formal courts. The two most popular competitive judicial debate formats are mock trial debate and moot court debate. Both formats are used in law schools to train prospective lawyers. However, moot court and mock trial options are increasingly being offered to younger student competitors.

Neither mock trial nor moot court feature the use of a resolution. Rather, these debates are guided by the particular circumstances of a court case. The debaters take on the role of lawyers. Mock trial debate typically simulates a jury or bench trial. Moot court debate tends to revolve around arbitral or appellate court cases. The closest association to other debate forms would be that the affirmative is the prosecuting side and the negative is the side offering the defense.

Special Debate

Special debate formats are organized for specific events. As a result, they may or may not involve the use of a resolution. As an alternative to the use of a resolution, special debates may be moderated by one or more people posing questions to the debaters. In such cases, the moderator is responsible for keeping the participants limited to speaking within their allocated amounts of time and for keeping the debate moving forward. Special debates can often cover a wide range of topics.

One common example of a special debate is a debate organized to feature political candidates just prior to an election. Historically in the United States, presidential candidates from the major parties have engaged in three televised debates leading up to the election. Vice presidential candidates also engage in one televised debate. Within the context of political elections, these debates serve the very important function of allowing voters to learn more about the candidates prior to Election Day.

Another specialized form of debate is town hall. Town hall debate is defined primarily by its format. Within a town hall debate, participants sit in a hall surrounded by members of the audience. Over the course of the debate, members of the audience take turns asking the candidates questions. Often, the organizers of these debates prescreen the questions, but the audience members still enjoy the opportunity to engage the debaters directly. During a town hall format, the debaters often walk around the room in order to make eye contact with the different members of the audience.

Conclusion

Debate is rhetoric and argument in action. The content of a debate is guided by the presence of a resolution, a normative statement. Resolutions are used to guide the development of claims, or the conclusion of arguments. Good claims are bolstered by warrants, which are the reasoning or evidence that support the claim.

The resolution outlines different responsibilities to the competing debaters. The side supporting the resolution wording as part or wholly true is the affirmative. The affirmative team has the burden of proof. The negative must then argue against the affirmative's claims in order to meet its burden of rejoinder.

Competitive debate structures vary by number of participants. Debates can feature one debater arguing against another or a team of debaters competing against another team. The structure of debate is also influenced by the wording of the resolution. The resolution may endorse a policy action or a values statement. The type of resolution leads to participation in either policy or values debate. The wide range of debate formats, including policy debate, values debate, parliamentary debate, and moot court, illustrate how the resolution's wording can lead to very different methods of competitive argumentation.

Key Terms

Affirmative—The side of the debate responsible for defending the resolution.

Argument—A set of statements, one of which serves as a conclusion, while the others together provide support for that conclusion.

Backing—The evidence used to illustrate that the warrant is true.

Burden of Proof—The burden to prove or defend the resolution. Within a competitive debate, the burden of proof is typically assigned to the affirmative.

Burden of Rejoinder—The negative's burden to answer the affirmative. This burden only applies after the affirmative has fulfilled its burden of proof.

Claim—The conclusion of the argument being advanced by a debater.

Clash—A feature of debate in which both sides of the debate are discussing the same arguments and issues.

Debate—A structured deliberation in which opponents argue opposing viewpoints.

Grounds—the reasoning used to support the claim.

Mock Trial Debate—Legal debate format commonly used in law school that simulates a jury or bench trial.

Moot Court Debate—Legal debate format commonly used in law school that simulates an arbitral or appellate court trial.

Negative—The side of the debate responsible for arguing against the resolution.

Parliamentary Debate—A competitive debate format governed by the rules of parliamentary procedure.

Parametricize—The process of selecting an example of a resolution for the subject of debate, undertaken by the affirmative and most commonly practiced with policy resolutions.

Persuasion—The act of attempting to influence an individual's or group's attitudes, behaviors, beliefs, intentions, or motivations.

Policy Resolution—A type of resolution that identifies a policy action that should be undertaken.

Policy Debate—A type of debate format in which the debaters debate issues of policy and utilize a policy resolution.

Proposition—A declarative statement, containing subject and a predicate, that is either true or false.

Resolution—A normative statement that outlines the subject of the debate.

Rhetoric—Persuasion, the act of attempting to influence an individual's or group's attitudes, behaviors, beliefs, intentions, or motivations.

Status Quo—The present or existing status of things.

Values Resolution—A type of resolution that offers a statement of a value that ought to be advocated.

Values Debate—A type of debate format in which the debaters debate the intellectual endorsement of values and utilize a values resolution.

Warrant—the reason why the provided grounds supports the advanced claim.

Check Your Understanding

What is the relationship between rhetoric, persuasion, and argument?

What is the relationship between the resolution and the claim?

What is the difference between policy and value resolutions?

What are the responsibilities of the affirmative side?

What are the responsibilities of the negative side?

What is the "burden of rejoinder"?

What is clash?

What are the basics of LD debate?

What are the basics of Policy debate?

What are the basics of Parliamentary debate?

8 Preparing to Debate

Chapter Objectives

Preparing for your first debate is a thrilling experience. You know that you will be competing against another student (or two), and you know the general topic thanks to the resolution. From the resolution, you can craft a wide range of arguments, both negative and affirmative. In fact, if you are competing at a tournament, you will need to prepare to argue both sides of the resolution. Even if you are only debating for one round in a class, you can substantially improve your performance by familiarizing yourself with the arguments that your opponent is likely to raise.

After reading this chapter, you will be able to:

- Research a topic
- Assemble affirmative arguments
- Assemble negative arguments
- Distinguish the key features of the three types of speeches in a debate round
- Flow a debate
- Identify the key features of a debate used by judges to determine the winner
- Discuss a practice round

This information is critical to the pre-tournament preparation that all debaters should complete prior to participating in their first debate round. This chapter provides guidance on how to prepare to debate. Due to the higher level of difficulty and complexity found within policy debate rounds, this chapter's content as well as the content of the next two chapters will discuss primarily policy debate preparation. However, much of the information will also apply to values debate rounds.

Researching for Your Debate

It is essential that you fully research a given topic. This means you need to know both sides of the issue to be able to defend or oppose it fully. Scholarly sources should be your number one choice. Log on to your library's online journal database and use key words to find numerous articles on your topic and valid and reliable statistics. News organizations are solid choices but keep in mind that there are some new sources that have been deemed biased and/or slanted that may weaken your argument's credibility (ethos). Evaluate all your sources for credibility (ethos). If your source is lacking in credibility your arguments may not be as persuasive.

Where to Research

Library

Your local library and your college or university library will have access to a plethora of scholarly articles and credible sources of information. The library is an excellent place to start researching your topic. The library carries articles, books, newspapers, periodicals, magazines, encyclopedias, films, the list goes on and on. If you are unfamiliar with how to search for books, journals, and newspapers in nearby libraries, ask the librarians to help you get started. Librarians will be eager to assist you. You can find books, articles, newspapers, and really old materials of all kinds at the library.

Internet

A significant amount of research these days are done over the Internet. Most schools have an online database for articles that is amazing! Use it! Most schools allow you to access the library from home computers as well as school computers. Otherwise you can use other research-based search engines, such as Google or Yahoo. These searches will provide you with some relevant and some not-so-relevant websites. Use your best judgment and the criteria for assessing sound sources to establish whether or not that particular data is a good idea to use. Google Scholar is potentially an adequate source for finding articles in scholarly journals, though subscriptions may be required for some access and your college or local library will likely allow you free access.

The Research Process

The research process is simple. You first need to distinguish your key words, find sources, evaluate the sources, collect reference information, and organize your research.

Key Words and Phrases

First, type the key words or even the entire resolution into your favorite basic and scholarly search engines. These results can give a very broad background on the types and availability of information that is most common. Read a few of these to get an overview of the topic. This will also help in defining any confusing terms. Be sure to pay attention to the diversity of perspectives. Being well rounded and understanding the topic fully is key to winning a debate. Your ability to refute an opponent well is highly dependent on your ability to know what is likely to be brought up during a debate.

Distinguish the Types of Evidence Needed

Second, you need to establish what kinds of evidence you will need and how that evidence will need to be used during the debate. The goal of most of your research is to find evidence, data, and information that support your claims. You will need different evidence depending on your topic and side. Decide what type of evidence you will need for your speech. Use the questions below to guide you.

1. Do I need examples?
2. Do I need testimony?
3. Do I need reasoning and logic?
4. Do I need explanation and visual depictions?
5. Do I need expert opinion?
6. Do I need a specific statistic?
7. Do I need several statistics on the same idea over a period of time?
8. Do I need scholarly evidence?
9. Do I need government-based evidence?
10. Do I need to provide basic definitions for any concepts?
11. What evidence is essential to make my point?
12. What evidence can I use that will pack the biggest punch?

13. Do I need to know more generally?
14. Do I need to appeal to pathos through stories?

You will need to define the critical terms in your debate, which means you need to research the definitions of various terms. Choose dictionaries that have credibility to them and also consider how you might defend a definition that is not necessarily the denotative definition of the word and do the necessary research. Definition of key terms is very important to your case. Often you will read these definitions aloud; however, sometimes you may not, it will depend on the particular case and how using the definition will suit your case.

When you present your case, if you do not read your definitions, you must still include them in your cards and brief. You may say, "As the affirmative team we reserve the right to clarify any definitions throughout this round" which gives you the ability to come back and define terms that you may not have defined in the first speech. Additionally, you always properly "cite" or state your definitions.

Discern Good from Bad Evidence

Third, you will want to make sure the evidence you found is good. What is good evidence? Please consider the following criteria and see the hierarchy of evidence diagrams to help you discern what is and is not quality evidence. Evaluate your evidence in the following areas:

Relevance: Using irrelevant information weakens your ethos as a speaker and your argument. Ensure the evidence is relevant and directly connected to your argument.

Generalizability: The sample must be representative of the population. For instance, let us say you find a study that found eight out of ten teenagers in America admit to smoking cigarettes before the legal age. You need to look at the sample size of that research to know if it is generalizable. If the study was a sample of 30 teens from a Los Angeles city high school, the findings are not generalizable because 30 teens from the city do not reflect the greater population of the United States, which has cities, farming areas, rural areas, and significantly more than 30 teens.

Recency: Any information you gather from any kind of source should be no more than ten years old. The only exception to this rule is if you are using evidence or a source intended for an argument based in tradition. For example, you may want to quote a historical document, such as the Bill of Rights or the Declaration of Independence. Clearly, these sources are more than ten years old, but they are the exception to the rule. You also want to determine if there is more current information available. If so, you need to find out whether that information is similar or dissimilar to your less-recent evidence.

Credibility: Credibility concerns perceptions of competence, ethics, fairness, intelligence, reputation, and good will. There are two types of credibility: direct and secondary. **Direct credibility** is support you create yourself. An example of direct credibility is any time you mention your own personal experience or expertise. **Secondary credibility** is support you generate by using other people's credibility. For example, you may not be an expert in astrophysics, so you choose to cite an expert in the field instead. You are basically borrowing credibility.

Trustworthiness: When considering whether or not a piece of evidence is trustworthy, consider the reputation of the source. Does the person or organization have a positive track record of being trustworthy, ethical, and unbiased? If it is a secondary source that you are considering using, ask yourself, "does it accurately and fully represent the original source's findings?" Determine whether the source is biased or not. One way to determine prejudice or bias is to consider who collected the data, and who paid for the research.

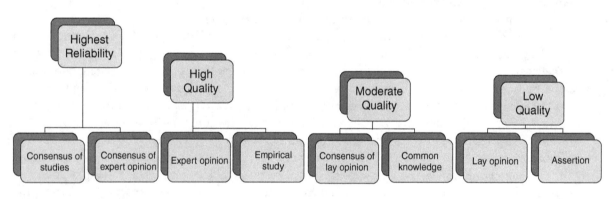

Get Organized

Fourth you will want to establish a system of organization. Once you have determined what type of evidence you need, you can start researching! But, before you get carried away and begin stacking up the books and scrolling through pages on the Internet, you need to have a way to organize your research efforts. This is a step many first-time speakers and researchers skip. Often students tell themselves, "Oh, I'll remember where that quote was" or "I'll figure out the citation information later." These procrastination moments can cost you several hours of time later on. It is best to start your research with a clear idea of what you are looking for, how you are going to use it, and how you are going to keep track of it. There are three principles to follow when organizing your information: copy important material, craft a working reference page, and file in an organized fashion.

1. **Copy the material.** This does not mean you have to copy all 300 pages of a book, but it does mean you should copy the page in which your quote/statistic/information occurs. Once you have the copy

made, you need to highlight and/or underline the piece of information you will use so that you can quickly and efficiently locate the information later. You also want to note on that copy exactly where in your speech this evidence will be used (introduction, conclusion, or one of the main points).

2. **Create a working reference page.** Most people wait until the last minute to start their reference page. This is a big mistake. You want to create a working reference page as you go, so that when you make your reference page, you are not struggling and stressed to find the source and locate all the pertinent information. I should note that not all instructors require a reference page. You should clarify your instructor's expectations. You should also clarify with your instructor as to which style or citing sources they would like you to use. The American Psychological Association (APA) is the official form of citing in the communication discipline, but again clarifies the exact expectations of your instructor. Keep in mind that regardless of the official style of citing you use for your written work, your oral citations (which will be discussed later) always require the author's name and year at minimum. For your reference page you will need: the author's name, the organization's name (if one is affiliated with the person or the study), the publisher's name, the date it was published, the date the study was conducted (if it was a study), the title of the work, and where you gathered it from and when.

3. **File documents in one central place and use distinguishing tabs.** Once you have collected all this information, the last thing you want to do is misplace pieces here and there. Have one dedicated file folder that you use only for the research on this particular topic and your days or weeks of researching and preparing will be worth it. Divide your evidence according to how it will be used in your case. For instance, if I am the affirmative I might have a file for "harm 1," "harm 2," and "harm 3." The evidence needed for different harms will be significant. Labeling and categorizing is essential. Be sure to use a means of organizing that works well for you.

Make Your Cards and Properly Cite

Fifth, you will use your files and make your cards, because during your debate you need to verbally cite your sources. For example, you might say "According to Thorson, Staller, & Korcok, 2013, page 132, "insert quote here," or give your statement and in the end give the author, year, and page number where the quote is found. The idea with citing your source is that you are proving that your evidence is credible, that you are not plagiarizing, that the source is current, and that others could easily find this information themselves. If you are taking college class ask your professor which formatting style they prefer. The American Psychological Association (APA) style is commonly used in the communication discipline and as such is what will be displayed in the examples below.

Examples of How You Will Verbally Cite Your Sources:

According to the book *Contemporary Public Speaking* by Thorson, Staller, & Korcok, 2013, page 213, "research can be divided into two categories."

Or

According to communication scholars Thorson, Staller, & Korcok in a public speaking textbook *Contemporary Public Speaking: How to Craft and Deliver a Powerful Speech*, published in 2013, "research can be divided into two categories" (p. 342).

Example of How You Will use In-Text Citations in Your Briefs:

"Research is a tool that benefits many different types of speeches. The goal of **research** is to aid you informing a solid case so that you and your arguments are more likely to be accepted by the audience.

If an audience is disappointed in your research efforts, it will significantly affect your ethos(credibility) for that speech. Research influences the effectiveness of the modes of persuasion that are critical to a speech. Failing to know the rules and expectations of research can also affect your logos(logic). And, finally, even your pathos(appeal to emotions) can be affected by poor research" (Thorson, Staller, Korcok, 2013, p. 92).

Citation rules change. Always check your most current manual, APA and MLA (Modern Language Association) are the most commonly used.

Cutting Cards

Using the articles you gathered, cut cards for your research and debates. Using cards during your debate will enable you to debate more efficiently. Each piece of evidence you find will need to be cut into a "card." The term "card" comes from the ancient days of debate (before the 1980's and computers) when most all debaters literally cut out quotes from original sources and pasted them onto single note cards. There would be one piece of evidence per card. Your card should have only one source's information on it. You can have multiple quotes, but only if they are all from that author, article, book, etc. Your instructors may vary slightly on their specific expectations regarding cards, what is offered here is a good starting template of what is commonly done in debate card making. Your card should contain the following information:

Tag line: a short, to the point 2–4-word summary of what the evidence presents. The tag line should be simple and accurate and quickly reflect the card's contents. Ultimately, the tag line should allow you to recall the information and use it in your debate as efficiently as possible.

Citation information: The author, publication details, page numbers for direct quotes, and the credibility of the author who offered the evidence. This information must be in APA format and will need to be verbally cited as well.

Underlined and or highlighted content: the essential and critical pieces of evidence should be underlined so that the reader can easily see the information. This should be the information you intend to use directly in your debate. During the debate these underlined portions of your card are the parts you will read aloud. The remainder of information serves as context if your opponents or the judge asks to see the card. You should have at minimum three sentences above and below the sentences you actually intend to use in the debate.

Your evidence cards have more information than you may actually need to read during a debate. For example, you do not normally need to read all of the credibility statement, but you should have this information in case your opponent or anyone asks questions about the reasonability of the evidence, the source, the author, or how the author arrived at his or her conclusions. Neither do you normally need to read the URL of your source, but it too is important to have available. The full source citation also makes it easier to prepare a bibliography if your professor requires one.

Please see the example:

Tax increases lower economic growth a lot

Romer and Romer 2010   (Christina & David, economics professor at Berkeley & chair President Obama's Council of Economic Advisors 20092010 & economics professor at Berkeley and NBER, American Economic Review, The Macroeconomic effects of Tax Changes, June 2010)

"Our results indicate that tax changes have very large effects on output. Our baseline specification implies that an exogenous tax increase of one percent of GDP lowers real GDP by almost three percent. Our many robustness checks for the most part point to a slightly smaller decline, but one that is still typically over 2.5 percent. In addition, we find that the output effects of tax changes are much more closely tied to the actual changes in taxes than to news about future changes, and that investment falls sharply in response to exogenous tax increases."

Assembling Arguments

As discussed in the previous chapter, the affirmative team has the burden of proof while the negative team has the burden of rejoinder. These different burdens help to distinguish the types of arguments that debaters will prepare for when they speak on either side of the resolution.

Affirmative Preparation

The First Affirmative Constructive

The affirmative speech offers the first debate in the round: the first affirmative constructive. The affirmative also knows what the resolution is in advance. These two facts are tremendously important competitive advantages for the affirmative side of a debate. The affirmative team has a nearly infinite amount of time to prepare for the debate. As a result of these factors, much of the affirmative's preparation will revolve around writing the first affirmative constructive. The first affirmative constructive is the only speech in a debate round to be written entirely in advance. By writing your speech in advance, you can get up and simply read the speech as the means of starting the round.

In order to discuss the structural components of the first affirmative constructive, it is useful first to discuss a bit of debate history. Early formal debate competitions identified **stock issues** as the deliberative components of the affirmation of the resolution. The five stock issues are inherency, harms, significance, solvency, and topicality. First of all, **inherency** is the status quo. Inherency demonstrates that there is an issue that should be addressed but that the status quo is currently failing to address.

Three types of inherency may exist. **Structural inherency** is the legal barriers, such as laws, to action. **Attitudinal inherency** reflects the status quo belief of the public or of influential political attitudes that action is not needed. **Existential inherency** claims neither attitudinal nor structural barriers to action. It simply states that the harms exist and that the status quo is not addressing the harms, so something must be done.

Harms quantify the negative aspects of the status quo's failure to act. Harms and significance are closely linked. **Significance** is the demonstration that the harms are important enough to warrant action. Significance is proven by comparing the advantages of the affirmative's proposed action to the outcome expected from the status quo's inaction.

The fourth stock issue is solvency. **Solvency** defines the outcome of the affirmative's plan. It means that the affirmative's endorsed policy will solve the identified harms.

Finally, **topicality** is the characteristic of the plan that states that the affirmative's advocated plan is an example of the resolution. Remember, the duty of the affirmative is to defend the resolution. Within a policy round, the affirmative will parametricize, or select an example of the resolution, to promote as an option to be adopted. If the plan offered by the affirmative is not an example of the resolution, then all of the other stock issues no longer matter. The plan may be a good idea but it is not an example of the resolution.

Initially, stock issues were used directly as criteria for determining whether an affirmative should win the round. If an affirmative failed to meet one or more of the stock issues, then the negative would win the round. Today, however, stock issues are viewed by many contemporary debaters and coaches as outmoded concepts. With the exception of topicality, the stock issues are rarely discussed within debate rounds as a reason to vote against the affirmative plan. Nevertheless, knowledge of stock issues is important because stock issues continue to influence how the first affirmative constructive is prepared.

The first affirmative constructive (1AC) typically contains four parts. The first part of the 1AC describes the status quo. That description may address issues of inherency, harms, and significance to show that there is a problem that is not currently being addressed.

The second part of the 1AC is the plan. The **plan** details the proposal that the affirmative wants to pass. It is the affirmative's proposed course of action. The plan is also the affirmative's example of the resolution. The plan is the only part of the first affirmative constructive that does not contain evidence. Instead, it is entirely written by the affirmative debaters, often with the help of their coach or other debaters.

The plan is typically followed by either solvency or advantages. The **solvency** section of the first affirmative constructive provides evidence that shows that the course of action proposed within the plan will solve the outlined harms. The **advantages** outline the positive consequence of adopting the plan. Some first affirmative constructives do not outline advantages and instead focus attention upon the harms outlined in the first section as evidence that the plan is a good idea.

First Affirmative Constructive: A General Outline

A. Contention 1: The Status Quo
   Evidence showing inaction
   Evidence showing harms
B. The Plan
C. Contention 2: Solvency
   Evidence showing that the Plan will work
D. Contention 3: One or More Advantages
   (Optional)

   Advantages may also be included as part of the first contention, combined with the harms and inherency

---

Affirmative Blocks

In addition to the first affirmative constructive, the affirmative should also prepare for a debate round by preparing answers for the arguments that the affirmative expects the negative to raise during a round. These prepared answers are known as blocks. **Blocks** typically contain many different answers of different types. Blocks should include some evidence to support at least some of the answers as well.

This component of preparation is quite challenging. Affirmatives may expect negatives to argue things that they do not bring up. Affirmatives may also fail to predict particular arguments. Nevertheless, preparation for arguments likely to be raised is a wise strategic decision for the affirmative. Also, affirmatives should know their plan better than their opponents. This knowledge will allow debaters to know both the strengths and weaknesses of their first affirmative constructive. This knowledge should direct the preparation of blocks. Having answers prepared for likely arguments can save valuable preparation time and will also show the judge that the affirmative came prepared to debate.

Negative Arguments

Topicality

Topicality is often the first argument taught to novice debaters. As noted in the previous section, topicality is one of the stock issues. Topicality is the characteristic of the affirmative being an appropriate representation of the resolution. When the negative argues that the affirmative is not topical, the negative is arguing that the affirmative has failed to meet its essential duty to affirm the resolution.

A topicality argument is generally advanced in four parts. The first part defines a word of the resolution. The second part then argues that the plan text fails to meet that definition. This is the violation and the reason that the affirmative is not meeting its burden to defend the resolution.

The third section includes the standards for the evaluation of this argument. Common standards include grounds and fairness. For example, a fairness standard would argue that the affirmative must be topical in order to have a fair debate because negatives are expected to prepare arguments against plans that are topical.

The final part of a topicality argument is the voting issue. Within a debate round, topicality is an **a priori** issue. This means that it comes before all other considerations. Negatives argue that the judge must evaluate topicality first because non-topical affirmative plans do not matter because they do not support the resolution. If the negative wins topicality, the negative wins the round.

Topicality Argument Outline

A. Definition: Evidence, such as a definition from a dictionary
B. Violation: An explanation of why the plan does not meet the definition
C. Standards for evaluating the violation
D. Voting issue

More than one topicality violation can be argued by the negative team in the same round.

Disadvantages

Disadvantages are another common negative argument. A **disadvantage** argues that the plan will cause something bad to occur. They are typically advanced during the first negative constructive. If the disadvantage outweighs, or is more serious than, the advantages of the plan, the negative can argue that the affirmative's plan is a bad idea and that the judge should reject the plan by voting negative.

Disadvantages are composed of three parts and the negative must successfully argue all three parts in order to win the disadvantage. The first part of a disadvantage is uniqueness. **Uniqueness** demonstrates why the disadvantage will not occur absent the affirmative. If the disadvantage is not unique, it means that the negative consequences detailed by the disadvantage will occur regardless of plan passage. As a result, the disadvantage would not be a reason to reject passing the affirmative plan. Uniqueness is supported by a piece of timely evidence. The uniqueness part of a disadvantage is sometimes also called a brink because the negative argues that the plan pushes the status quo over the brink in order to cause the negative consequences of the disadvantage to occur uniquely.

The second part of a disadvantage is the link. The **link** argues that the affirmative plan will trigger or cause the disadvantage's negative impacts. The link demonstrates the connection between the plan's action and the disadvantage. The link is supported by evidence that is as specific as possible to the affirmative's recommended plan.

The third part of a disadvantage is the **impact**. The impact describes the negative consequences that will occur once the link is triggered. Again, the impact(s) of the disadvantage should be stated and then supported by evidence.

Sample Disadvantage Outline

A. Uniqueness/Brink
B. Link
C. Impact

As with topicality, the negative team can elect to run more than one disadvantage in the same round.

Counterplans

A **counterplan** is a policy option that is different from the plan. The negative offers the counterplan as a competitive policy alternative to the plan. To win the debate round, the negative must show that the counterplan is competitive with the plan and that the adoption of the counterplan is somehow better than the adoption of the affirmative plan.

The basic outline of a counterplan is divided into three parts: the counterplan text, competition, and solvency. Each of these three parts must be presented by the negative and will typically be presented in the first negative constructive. Counterplans may also include two optional components: conditionality and topicality.

Some debaters elect to include an optional component outlining the advantages of the counterplan. However, advantages of the counterplan are often not found within the formal outline of the counterplan and instead are argued elsewhere within the debate. Often, the advantages of the counterplan are presented as disadvantages. In fact, a common strategy used by negatives is to present a counterplan combined with a disadvantage that links to the plan and not the counterplan.

Counterplan Text

The **text of the counterplan** explains what the counterplan will do. It describes the negative's alternative course of action and the proposed opportunity cost of the plan. The negative's counterplan text will often emulate the format and language of the affirmative plan.

Competition

A counterplan must be competitive. In a debate round, competition means that there is a reason for the judge to choose the counterplan over the plan, and therefore vote negative instead of affirmative. The section on **competition** illustrates why a forced choice exists between the plan and the counterplan. An **opportunity cost** is the best option that must be foregone to adopt a posited action. The concept of opportunity cost is explored in greater detail in chapter nine. However, for the purposes of understanding the basic idea of a counterplan, remember this: If the counterplan is not competitive, it cannot be the plan's opportunity cost because it does not provide a reason not to do the affirmative since both the plan and the counterplan could be undertaken together.

Counterplan competition is described in one of two ways. The first type of competition is mutual exclusivity. **Mutual exclusivity** means that it is impossible for the plan and the counterplan to be undertaken together. Only one option may be selected because it is simply impossible to do both.

The second type of counterplan competition is net benefits. This form of competition is more complicated than mutual exclusivity. **Net benefits** means that doing the counterplan alone is better than doing both the plan and the counterplan. It may be possible to combine the plan and the counterplan, or the plan plus elements of the counterplan. However, any combination involving the whole plan and one or more parts of the counterplan are not as advantageous as passing the counterplan alone.

Standard Outline of a Counterplan

A. Counterplan text
B. Competition
C. Solvency with one or more pieces of evidence
    Optional Components:
        Conditionality
        Topicality

Solvency

The solvency section of the counterplan demonstrates that the plan will achieve the positive results. This section of the counterplan is similar to the affirmative plan's section on solvency. It should include one or possibly more pieces of evidence supporting the action proposed by the counterplan text. The solvency evidence may also include reasons to support the counterplan's competition.

Conditionality

Conditionality describes the state of the negative's advocacy of the counterplan. In a standard debate round, the affirmative's advocacy of the plan is considered nonconditional. This means that the affirmative team must advocate the affirmative plan throughout the debate round in order to win. The affirmative cannot choose to concede the plan and still win the round.

In contrast, negatives often argue that their advocacy of a counterplan is conditional rather than nonconditional. This status means that the negative team can opt out of arguing for the passage of the plan. This strategic move allows the negative team to revert back to defending the status quo. Some negatives may even decide to advance a different counterplan.

This textual component of the counterplan details whether the counterplan is conditional or nonconditional. This section may also indicate conditions that would allow the negative team to kick the counterplan and revert back to defending the status quo.

Topicality

A final, optional component of the counterplan is a discussion of its topicality. When counterplans were first advanced in competitive debate, they were presented as needing to be nontopical. After all, the affirmative team is supposed to prove that the resolution is true. If the counterplan also represents an example of the resolution, a good counterplan would appear to indicate that the resolution is a good idea. The negative team would essentially fulfill the role of the affirmative.

However, attitudes about the topicality status of counterplans have changed. Most judges agree that counterplans can be topical. This view is based upon the idea that once the affirmative selects a plan, the negative team should get to test that plan using all competitive options, both topical and nontopical.

Case Arguments

Negatives should also prepare arguments to answer directly the issues raised by the first affirmative constructive. Again, the stock issues can provide a guide on what sorts of arguments to make. For example, the negative can argue that the affirmative plan does not have solvency. This argument means that passage of the plan would still allow the harms to continue, making the passage of the plan a waste of time. The negative can also argue that the harms are not significant or that the status quo is acting to solve the problem already.

Case arguments are typically not enough to win a round for the negative by themselves. However, case arguments are a strong way to make the negative's counterplan and disadvantages more effective. Therefore, negatives should not neglect to answer the affirmative constructive's arguments. Ideally, these arguments should be backed by evidence. However, case arguments can also be effective without evidence.

Constructives, Rebuttals, and Cross-Examination

A debate round consists of three types of speeches: the constructives, the rebuttals, and the cross-examination. Each type is distinguished by length and content. Prior to competing in a tournament, debaters should familiarize themselves with the standard expectations and times assigned to these speeches.

Constructives

Constructive speeches have the longest duration of any speech within a debate round. They occur first in the debate. They are the only type of speech in which the debaters are allowed to present new arguments.

From these characteristics, constructives derive their name because debaters construct their arguments during these early speeches.

Rebuttals

Rebuttals occur later in a speech. They are shorter in length than the constructives. Debaters are also discouraged from making new arguments during the rebuttals. Instead, the purpose of rebuttals is to rebut the other side's arguments.

Rebuttals also have another very important but often-overlooked purpose: to explain why the side wins the round. The speech offered by both sides should answer the arguments raised by the other side. However, they should also explain why the judge should vote affirmative or negative.

Cross-Examination

Cross-examination periods allow debaters to ask their opponents direct questions. Cross-examination periods are typically brief. They are the shortest speeches in the round. They often last one, two, or three minutes. However, the information gained during the cross-examination period can be vital to determining the round's winner. Therefore, debaters should plan for their cross-examination period.

Flowing a Debate

The burden of rejoinder requires one debater to respond to the arguments raised by another. The failure to respond leads to dropped arguments, which are treated as concessions. Therefore, debates must take careful and complete notes of the content of the speeches offered by their opponents in order to ensure that they meet their burden of rejoinder. The note-taking strategy most commonly used by competitive debaters is called "flowing."

The flow sheet is a graphical representation of the content of the debate round. An empty flow sheet for a team policy debate round prior to the start of the round is shown below. The flow sheet is created by turning a sheet of paper horizontally and drawing lines to distinguish vertical columns. Each column is devoted to one speech. To take notes, the debater fills the column assigned to each speech, writing vertically.

Flow Sheet

1AC	1NC	2AC	2NC	1NR	1AR	2NR	2AR

Evaluating a Debate

Dropped arguments are often a very important component of a judge's evaluation of a debate. Judges who flow expect an argument to be answered in the speech after it is raised. An argument is considered dropped if it is raised by one side and not answered by the other side. When an argument is dropped, it is considered conceded by the other team. In other words, that argument is treated as if it is true and correct simply because it did not receive a response.

Practice

In order to get better at a particular sport, athletes engage in practice. Musicians also practice their musical instruments regularly. Similarly, debaters get better with practice. Practice allows debaters to get over any existing fear of public speaking. Practice also allows debaters to work out their "rap" or the way that they will present arguments and frame debate. Practice helps debaters to sound smooth and practiced, instead of struggling to find the correct word to use in a round.

Specifically, debaters will often organize practice rounds with their coaches or other debaters acting as judges. Debaters can participate in a practice round against members of their debate squad or, rarely, they will debate against debaters from another school to practice. Sometimes, if no other debater is available, a debate coach will even participate in a debate round as a debater.

A practice round emulates the practices used in a standard debate round. The debaters time themselves or rely upon the judge for timing. They keep to the times of speeches, ask questions in cross-examination, and explain why they should win. Engaging in practice rounds helps debaters to feel familiar with exactly how participation in a debate round feels. Practice rounds are also an excellent opportunity to gather feedback about particular arguments, to determine what works and what does not.

Conclusion

Pre-round preparation is a complicated process. Debaters must prepare arguments to be presented when affirmative and negative. Affirmatives plan and write out their entire first affirmative constructive prior to the start of the debate round. They should also prepare answers to the arguments that they expect the negative will use within a round. Negative teams must try to guess what the affirmative will discuss and often prepare by constructing arguments that will apply to a wide range of plans. Common negative arguments include topicality, disadvantages, and counterplans.

Debaters should also understand the structure of a debate round. While time limits differ across tournaments and debate organizations, all debates generally feature three types of speeches. Constructives are the longest speech in a debate round. They occur early and may include new arguments. Rebuttals occur later in the round, are shorter in length than constructives, and may not include new arguments. The purpose of a rebuttal speech is to answer the other side's arguments. The third type of speech is the cross-examination, a more relaxed block of time that is used to gather information and clarify points by asking direct questions to the competition.

Debaters and judges keep track of the arguments in a debate round by flowing. While traditionally flowing was conducted using a pen and paper, many contemporary debaters prefer to flow a speech using a computer. Judges use their flows to determine the winner of a round. Constructives and rebuttals are both flowed speeches while cross-examinations are commonly not flowed, although the answers in a cross-examination are considered binding.

Debaters interested in improving their performance prior to a round should consider participating in a practice debate round. Preparation rounds follow the rules of a standard debate round without the competitive environment. Practice rounds enable debaters to practice flowing, evaluate the strength of their arguments, and practice what they will say during a competitive round against opponents from other squads.

Key Terms

A Priori—An issue considered before all other arguments in the debate room, typically argued to support a vote on topicality.

Attitudinal Inherency—The status quo belief of the public or of influential political attitudes that action is not needed.

Blocks—Prepared answers to an anticipated argument.

Constructive—The longest type of speech in the debate; debaters may introduce new arguments and evidence.

Cross-Examination—The shortest speech in a debate and typically unflowed, gives the debaters the opportunity to ask questions, clarify points, examine the other team's evidence, and entertain the judge.

Disadvantage—A negative argument that illustrates a harm directly caused by the plan.

Dropped Argument—An argument raised by one debater and not answered by the opponent; dropped arguments are conceded and treated by most judges as if they are true.

Existential Inherency—A type of inherency that states that the harms exist and that the status quo is not addressing the harms, so something must be done.

First Affirmative Constructive—The first speech in a debate round, which explains how the affirmative team supports the resolution; the only speech to be entirely written in advance of the round.

First Negative Constructive—The first speech offered by the negative.

Flow Sheet—A graphical representation used by debaters, judges, and viewers to track the content of a debate round.

Harms—The negative aspects of the status quo's failure to act.

Inherency—The stock issue that demonstrates that there is an issue that should be addressed but upon which the status quo is currently failing to act.

Impact—The third and final component of a disadvantage, it shows the negative consequences that will occur once the link is triggered.

Link—The second part of a negative disadvantage, shows that the affirmative plan will trigger or cause the disadvantage's negative impacts

Mutual Exclusivity—The type of counterplan competition that argues that it is impossible to do both the plan and the counterplan.

Net Benefits—The type of counterplan competition that argues that the counterplan alone is better than doing both the plan and the counterplan.

Opportunity Cost—The best option that must be foregone in order to undertake a particular action or decision.

Plan—The component of the first affirmative constructive that describes the affirmative team's course of action.

Practice Round—An organized, noncompetitive debate round organized to allow debaters to work on skills and evaluate their arguments before engaging in formal competition.

Rebuttal—The second, shorter type of speech in a debate round; the debater is expected to answer existing arguments and avoid making new arguments.

Solvency—The stock issue that states that the affirmative plan, if passed, will solve the identified harms.

Stock Issues—the deliberative components of the affirmation of the resolution.

Structural Inherency—The legal barriers, such as laws, to action within the status quo.

Topicality—The characteristic of the plan that states that the affirmative's advocated plan is an example of the resolution.

Uniqueness—The first part of a disadvantage, demonstrates why the disadvantage will not occur absent the affirmative.

Check Your Understanding

What questions should you ask to determine the type of evidence you need for your debate?

1.

2.

3.

4.

5.

6.

7.

8.

9.

10.

11.

12.

13.

14.

When you evaluate evidence there are five main criteria you must consider. Name them and describe them please.

1.

2.

3.

4.

5.

Please rank research/data/ sources in order from most reliable and credible to least reliable and credible and define them.

1.

2.

3.

4.

5.

6.

7.

8.

What are the three principals of organizing your research?

1.

2.

3.

When you verbally cite your sources what information should you ensure you mention?

What is a tag line and how long should it be?

What information should always be on a card?

What are stock issues?

Define and describe the three types of inherency.

1.

2.

3.

What are advantages and who produces them?

What are disadvantages and who produces them?

What is topicality?

What are the three parts of a disadvantage and what do they mean?

1.

2.

3.

What is a counterplan specifically and what do you need to consider when crafting one?

What is conditionality?

What is the difference between a constructive and a rebuttal?

How is a cross-examination used during debates?

What should you consider when judging, evaluating, and flowing a debate?

Orally Citing Your Sources Worksheet

This worksheet will help you construct your oral citations for your speech and your APA citation for your reference page. You will need two pieces of evidence for this activity. You may use scholarly research or statistics from credible sources for this activity. Be sure to refresh the earlier pages that explain how to orally cite your sources. Use the reference information to construct your citations.

Evidence #1: Title of Work:

Author:

Credibility of the author (credentials):

Year published:

Publisher:

Credibility of Publisher:

Page number the information is located. If no page number is present use the paragraph number:

The exact direct quote or paraphrased information you will be using from this source:

Oral Citation to be spoken during the speech:

APA Citation to be used in a reference page:

Evidence #2: Title of Work:

Author:

Credibility of the author (credentials):

Year published:

Publisher:

Credibility of Publisher:

Page number the information is located. If no page number is present use the paragraph number:

The exact direct quote or paraphrased information you will be using from this source:

Supporting Evidence Worksheet

For your speech you will need a variety of support. Make sure you have enough quality evidence, especially if you are giving a persuasive speech. Use this worksheet to help you practice how you will collect your data and analyze your evidence.

Evidence Support #1:

Title of Book/Article:

Author and Publisher/Journal:

Main Point/Claim this evidence will support:

What level of quality is this piece of evidence?

When was it published?   Is this "current" then?

Is this fully relevant to your point?

Is this source unbiased on this topic?

Is the evidence presented ethically?

Is the source credible and trustworthy?

Is this information generalizable?

If you answered "YES" to all the question the source has met the standards. Well done!

If your "level of quality" is of moderate or low quality consider adding a higher quality evidence to further support the claim in your speech.

If you answered "NO" to any of these questions your evidence has a weakness. If you have more than one "NO" you may not want to use the evidence at all. Consider ways you can either strengthen the argument further (get higher quality and credible sources in addition to this) or using the weakness as an asset (perhaps your "old" evidence works to compare a past result with a current result).

APA Citation to be used in any reference pages

Using Statistics in Your Speech

Statistics are facts or occurrences represented by numbers. Statistics work well for argumentative speeches because you are able to back up abstract generalizations with specific data. Statistics can be used to quantify information, demonstrate trends, and establish cause-effect relationships.

Remember that your statistics are only as good as your sources: you should use unbiased, credible sources for your statistics. (Statistic from the NRA in a pro-gun speech would not be a wise choice if you were speaking to a liberal audience.)

Mark Twain said that there were three kinds of lies, "Lies, damned lies, and statistics." My favorite anonymous quotation for statistics: "Statistics are like bikinis—what they reveal are interesting, but what they conceal are vital." In other words, human beings know that number can be manipulated, so it is a good idea to combine your statistics with other kinds of verbal support, like expert testimony or logical argumentation.

Hints for using statistic effectively:

1. Make sure your statistic are representative. Interviewing ten students on a campus is not a large enough sample to make any statistical claims about the general opinions of the entire student population.

2. Build up the credibility of your source before presenting your statistic.

3. Round off your statistics to make them easier to remember. (Rather than saying, "Of the 493,975 people who smoke, 51.05 percent will contract some form of cancer," say, "Or the approximately one-half million people who smoke, about half will contract some form of cancer.")

4. Use statistics with intelligence, too many numbers will result in information overload, and your audience will experience the "Charlie Brown" effect: their brains will not be able to keep up, and all they will hear is "Wa wa wa wa."

5. When possible, provide visual aids to reinforce your statistics and aid in memory. (You can use bar graphs, pie charts, and other visual representations for numbers.)

6. Personalize your statistics and make them mean something to your audience. After presenting a statistic, provide an example to which your audience can relate. ("Last year five million tons of garbage was deposited in United States landfills. If you stacked this garbage three feet high, it would cover the entire states of Washington, Oregon, and California.")

Verbal Support: Example of Raw Research

True Story:
Health education teacher Pacy Erck remembers what it was like back when Edina High School students had to show up by 7:25 a.m. "The kids were always very tired," she recalls. But these days, Erck rarely has a kid nod off in class. That's because in the fall of 1996, officials at this Minnesota school decided to ring the first bell an hour later, at 8:30 a.m. *Sleep* researchers had reported that teens' natural slumber patterns favor a later bedtime, and the school wanted to ensure that its high schoolers weren't being shortchanged by an early *wake-up* call. The change means that students average five more hours of *sleep* a week, and teachers can see a difference. "You don't have the kids putting their heads down," Erck says. "The class is livelier" (Boyce).

Surprising Fact:
Most of all, losing sleep alters your metabolism, setting the stage for weight gain. Scientists at the University of Chicago have found that a sleep debt of three to four hours over a few days was all it took to provoke metabolic changes that mimicked pre-diabetes. The researchers monitored 11 healthy young adults for 16 consecutive nights in a clinical research center and found that when their sleep was restricted to four hours for six consecutive nights, their ability to keep blood glucose on an even keel declined significantly [Ward).

Expert Opinion:
Artificial light from computer and television screens tells the brain that it's not time to wind down. "Your body thinks artificial light is daylight—which prevents the release of melatonin, a *sleep*-inducing chemical," says Susan Zafarlotfi, PhD, director of the Institute for *Sleep*-Wake Disorders at Hackensack University Medical Center (Pagán).

Statistic:
A trimmer waistline. People who logged 7 to 9 hours a *night* had an average *BMI* of 24.8-almost 2 points lower than the average *BMI* of those who slept less, University of Washington researchers found. Too-little *sleep* may throw off *hormones* that regulate appetite (Winters).

Resource Activity: Citing Your Sources Worksheet

Directions: Using the resource (magazine, newspaper, book, etc.) provided to you, find a fact, statistic, example, testimony, or quote you might use as supporting material in a speech. Complete the form below to practice the three forms of citations.

Write the information you found to use in your speech below:

1. **Reference citation in APA format (this is the detailed reference for the list at the end of your outline):** *Note your entire reference list should be alphabetized by last name (or by title for articles or information with no author) with subsequent lines indented-called a "hanging in dentation."*

2. **Verbal citation (how would you "say it" in your presentation?) The following are a few examples:**
   "As reported by (author) in (publication) on (date)...
   "According to (author) in (publication) on (date)...
   "In the (date) edition of (publication), (author) argues...

3. **Internal Citation (how would you include this in your typed formal outline?)**
   Provide the information gleaned followed by the author's last name and year of publication in parenthesis OR write the line exactly how you are planning to verbally cite it (from #2 above)

Example of Paraphrased Research in Oral Citation Format

True Story:
In their May 17, 2004 US News and World Report article titled, "The Secrets of Sleep", Nell Boyce and Susan Brink tell the story of Pacy Erck, a Health Education teacher at Edina High School in Minnesota. Ms. Erck struggled for years to keep her morning students awake. She says they were "always nodding off". That is, until school officials made a change that helped all of the students at Edina High School get 5 more hours a week of sleep. The change was surprisingly simple: They moved the start of classes from 7:30 to 8:30 in the morning. Erck has seen a dramatic change. She says her students are no longer dropping their heads constantly and classes are "livelier."

Surprising Fact:
Elizabeth Ward reports some startling discoveries in her September, 2004 article for Environmental Nutrition, "Good night, sleep tight. Weight, immunity and memory will benefit,". Ward writes that sleep researchers at the University of Chicago found that missing just 3-4 hours of sleep nightly over less than a week sends people into a metabolic tailspin so severe that they begin to exhibit early signs of diabetes.

Expert Opinion:
In, "The Family Sleep Cure," published in the January 2009 edition of Prevention magazine writer Camille Noe Pagan reveals one cure she learned from Susan Zafarlotfi, PhD, director of the Institute for *Sleep-Wake* Disorders at Hackensack University Medical Center, that will help the whole family sleep. Zafarlotfi cautions that artificial lighting from TV and computer screens confuses our brains, making us think it is still daylight. This prevents the release of a chemical that helps us sleep, melatonin. As a result, we are wakeful, tossing and turning instead of getting the sleep we need.

Statistic:
Catherine Winters warns, in her February 2009 Prevention magazine article, "Sleep. It's non-negotiable", that a lack of sleep can also have a negative effect on our waistlines! She shares a University of Washington study that found that people who get a full night's sleep tend to have a BMI 2 points lower than people who skimp on sleep.

References

[These are not done in proper APA format-circle the errors]

Boyce, Nell & Brink, Susan. "THE SECRETS OF SLEEP." U.S. News & World Report 17 May 2004: 58-68.
Pagán, Camille Noe. "The Family Sleep Cure." Prevention 2009 January: 155-157.
Ward, Elizabeth M. "Good Night, Sleep Tight. Weight, Immunity And Memory Will Benefit." Environmental Nutrition September 2004: 1-6.

The 3 elements of each piece of evidence

1. The tagline

The tagline is a single sentence claim that you wish to make in a debate, which is supported by the quote. Taglines are not a summary or paraphrase of the quotation and they are not commentary or an evaluation of it either: they are the conclusion you wish to draw from the quotation.

Taglines should be short, memorable, and useful in a debate.

2. The source

The source usually has 2 components, the short part meant to be said in a debate and the details of the source, available if more information is needed.

The short part of the source meant to be said in a debate is usually just the last name of the author of the quote and the year the quote was published. Although the last name and year don't contain any details of or about the source, those aren't usually required at initial presentation. An opponent or judge can always ask about those details later.

The details of the source are typically included within parentheses after the author's last name and year of publication. They are included in case the author's qualifications, the credibility of the publication, or questions about the quote's authenticity become issues. This part of the source is often rather detailed, especially for important pieces of evidence.

3. The quote

The quote is a word-for-word quotation from the source, which supports the claim made in the tagline.

This part of a piece of evidence is not a paraphrase or a synopsis or an editorial comment, but rather a direct quotation of the author's words. Although using ellipses to skip over uninteresting portions of the text used to be a common practice, it is usually unacceptable these days. A debater isn't required to read the entire quote on the page in a debate, so highlighting or bolding the part of the quote one expects to read is the usual method.

An Example Piece of Evidence

Name: _____   Topic: _____   p. _____ of _____

Class: _____   Argument: _____

Taxes Lower Economic Growth

Romer and Romer 2010   (Christina & David, economics professor at Berkeley & chair President Obama's Council of Economic Advisors 2009-2010 & economics professor at Berkeley and NBER, American Economic Review, The Macroeconomic effects of Tax Changes, June 2010)

"Our results indicate that tax changes have very large effects on output. Our baseline specification implies that an exogenous tax increase of one percent of GDP lowers real GDP by almost three percent. Our many robustness checks for the most part point to a slightly smaller decline, but one that is still typically over 2.5 percent. In addition, we find that the output effects of tax changes are much more closely tied to the actual changes in taxes than to news about future changes, and that investment falls sharply in response to exogenous tax increases."

Negative Disadvantage Outline

A. Uniqueness -
Uniqueness demonstrates why the disadvantage will not occur absent the affirmative. Uniqueness is supported by a piece of timely evidence.

B. Link -
The link argues that the affirmative plan will trigger or cause the disadvantage's negative impacts. The link is supported by evidence, which is as specific as possible to the affirmative.

C. Impact -
The Impact describes the negative consequences that will occur once the link is triggered. Again, the impact(s) of the disadvantage should be stated and then supported by evidence.

Negative Counterplan Outline

A. Counterplan Text -
This section explains what the counterplan will do.
The counterplan text describes the negative's alternative course of action.

B. Competition -
This section explains why there is a forced choice between the plan and counterplan. One of two justifications are possible: Either Mutual Exclusivity (It is impossible to do both the plan and counterplan) or Net Benefits (the counterplan alone is better than doing both the plan and counterplan

C. Solvency -
This section demonstrates that the counterplan will achieve the positive results This section should include a piece of evidence or two

CHAPTER

9   One on One Debate

Chapter Objectives

What happens in a one on one debate? The previous chapter discussed the type of arguments likely to be raised in a debate round, such as the affirmative's plan and the negative's disadvantages. This chapter now turns to the process of debate. Within a round, debaters will engage in arguing the facts of a specific scenario constructed around the wording of the resolution. Debaters will also argue about how to properly evaluate an action. These types of arguments are all focused upon leading the judge to make a decision that will determine the round's victor in a favorable manner.

When you complete this chapter, you should be able to:

- Argue the facts of a case through the establishment of definitions, setting of criteria, and discussion of evidence
- Debate values by critiquing assumptions, arguing about ethics, and deliberating about institutions
- Describe the different approaches to evaluating action

Knowledge of these topics will help the debater to understand the issues found within the debate round and how to communicate to the judge about the issues at stake.

Arguing the Facts

Establishing Definitions

As discussed in the previous chapter, resolutional wording provides guidance for the content of the debate. However, words often have different meanings and disagreements about the appropriate meaning of the terms used within a resolution can lead to very different interpretations about what a debate round on a given resolution should look like. As a result, definitions are an important part of debate. Members of both sides want to define the terms of the resolution in a way that will support their interpretation of the resolution.

The initial responsibility for the establishment of definitions belongs to the affirmative. Within the first speech of the round, the affirmative may choose to define specific words from the resolution. Alternatively, many affirmatives will choose to operationally define the terms simply by presenting their case. An **operational definition** is the definition of the terms based upon their usage in the round.

Once the affirmative finishes the first speech, the negative has two options. First, the negative can accept the definitions offered by the affirmative and focus upon arguing other points of the case. Alternatively, the negative can decide to argue a definition that is different from the affirmative.

The most common example of the negative challenging the definitions established by the affirmative is the topicality argument discussed in the previous chapter. To support this argument, the negative would offer a counter definition of the resolutional term at issue. The negative would then argue reasons why the negative's definition is superior to the definition offered by the affirmative.

Initially, debates about the definition of a term may seem very boring and difficult to decide. Some words have multiple meanings, as any dictionary will confirm. However, debates about the establishment of definitions focus less upon the literal meaning and more about the impact of such definitions upon the quality of the debate round. Topicality and other definitional arguments are won and lost based upon the strength of interpretation.

Definitional debates are often about which side has the best interpretation of what a debate round should like look. Negatives will often argue for very limited and focused definitions. This interpretation limits the number of affirmative cases that can be run, which allows the negative to better prepare for the affirmative's arguments. The negative would argue that this interpretation promotes fairness by undermining some of the inherent advantages of being affirmative. The negative would also argue that a limited topic promotes clash because negatives can focus their time outside of rounds upon developing strategies against a limited number of affirmative plans, instead of developing general strategies that are less specific but that apply to a wider range of plan options.

In contrast, affirmatives will often argue that a broader interpretation of terms is best for debate. Broader definitions allow affirmatives more creativity in crafting a plan. As a result, debates are less likely to become boring because debaters can argue many different things in a round. Remember that most resolutions are used by debate organizations for one or two whole semesters, so having a resolution capable of sustaining a long series of debates is a priority. The affirmative would argue that competitive debate works best when the affirmative gets some leeway to be creative.

These conflicting views of definitions come down to whether a debater prefers depth or breadth within a debate round. Affirmatives strategically prefer breadth. Negatives, however, prefer depth and predictability. These arguments can all become the basis for a definitional debate over whether the affirmative's selection of a questionable topic promotes good or bad debate.

For example, the negative may feel that the affirmative interpreted one or more terms in a way that disadvantages the negative by enabling the affirmative to offer a plan inconsistent with the plain meaning or intent of the resolution. Therefore, the negative may argue topicality as a corrective to this affirmative excess. Instead of forcing the negative to argue against a nontopical plan, the negative would reason that the affirmative should lose the round.

Setting Criteria

Criteria are the standards upon which a debate decision is made. Criteria may be established within both policy and values debate rounds. The subject of criteria is typically first raised by the affirmative as a means of persuading the judge of the good created by endorsing the affirmative's advocacy. Within a value debate round, where criteria is most commonly discussed, the affirmative will argue for the support of their value based upon the outlined criteria. Within the context of the first affirmative constructive of a policy debate round, the criteria reinforces the importance of the plan's solvency of the stated harms.

For example, a common criterion for evaluation of a debate round is human survival. Within the context of this criterion, the affirmative will win the round if the affirmative plan saves the lives of more people than the status quo or the counterplan (if the negative chooses to argue one). Once the negative hears the affirmative's identification of the criterion of survival, the negative has the option to either argue within the context of the affirmative's selected criterion or offer a counter criterion. If the negative accepts the criterion of survival, the negative could aim to win the round by showing that the affirmative costs lives instead of saving them by running a disadvantage. Alternatively, the negative may choose to argue that the criterion of survival supports voting for the negative by arguing that the negative counterplan is competitive and saves more lives than the affirmative plan.

However, the negative does not have to accept the criteria outlined by the affirmative. Instead, the negative can offer a counter criterion, which is an alternative criterion that the negative believes should guide the judge's decision. To support the counter criterion, the negative will argue that the affirmative's criterion is problematic.

Discussing Evidence

The discussion of evidence is an important part of life outside of a debate round. Every day, individuals must make decisions about whether to accept a vaccination, make a purchase, or travel to a location. Difficult decisions are made based upon the availability of evidence, such as news reports and medical studies. In a debate round, **evidence** is the statistics, facts, and opinion used to support a debater's argument.

Evidence used in a debate round can be acquired from many different sources. Most evidence is taken from published resources, such as newspapers, magazines, journals, and books. However, evidence may also be collected from unpublished sources, such as unpublished manuscripts or personal emails. The quality of evidence varies considerably from author to author, source to source. Debaters should be prepared to evaluate, discuss, and even criticize evidence within a debate round.

One method of distinguishing between different pieces of evidence is to look at the date of publication. For arguments requiring recent information such as the uniqueness evidence of a negative disadvantage, evidence is frequently taken from newspapers, magazines, and journals. From one tournament to another, debaters are likely to update such arguments with more recent evidence. In such cases, a piece of evidence published in the last week can be argued to be superior to evidence published a year ago. Arguments less dependent upon timeliness may be taken from a broader collection of sources, including books, legal opinions from court cases, and government records. For such arguments, timeliness may still be a relevant consideration but it is not the most important factor distinguishing between pieces of evidence.

Evidence can also be distinguished by looking at the author's qualifications. **Expert evidence** is written by someone with professional or educational credentials that make the author a qualified expert. For example, evidence written by a professor and then published in a peer-reviewed academic journal would be considered expert evidence. Expert evidence is likely to be preferred when discussing difficult to understand or technical concepts. Lay evidence is authored by someone who is not an expert. Newspaper articles, for example, are often written by journalists with limited additional training or education.

Debating Values

Critiquing Assumptions

A **critique** is a disciplined method of analyzing oral or written discourse. Within a debate round, a critique often functions by challenging the assumptions that underlie speech acts. Debaters may argue that the assumptions made by the other side are so egregious that they should be considered in the judge's evaluation of who wins the round. Critiques are a popular form of debate argument and they are often raised first in a round by the negative. Debate critiques are sometimes alternatively spelled "kritics."

Many debate critiques challenge traditional power structures and draw upon the work of respected social, economic, and political critics. For example, Karl Marx's critical analysis focused upon economic power structures. Many postmodern critics, on the other hand, challenge dominant worldviews and the assumptions that are the foundation of those perspectives. Feminist criticism may argue that certain assumptions favor men, queer theorists may challenge heteronormativity, and racial critics may point to the factors that systematically grant white privilege.

Within a debate round, critiques may be directed towards the rhetoric of debaters or the assumptions of the authors read as evidence by the debaters. Some critiques are based upon the language choice of debaters. For example, those who fail to use gender-inclusive language may be accused of sexist language. Alternatively, criticism may be directed toward the realist assumptions made by policy authors who are read as evidence in a debate round.

Functionally, critiques are organized in a manner similar to a disadvantage. A critique argument must contain a link and an impact. However, critiques often do not attempt to argue uniqueness. For many critiques, the status quo likely links to the critique as much as the negative plan. Instead, critiques include a consideration of an alternative to the assumption being critiqued. The debaters advocating the critique will then argue that the judge's ballot indicates intellectual endorsement of that alternative over the problematic assumptions.

Critiques also provide a way for debaters to deliberate about the activities of institutions and public actors. Counterplans that involve action undertaken by actors other than the plan actor enable the negative to question the assumptions of relying upon state action. For example, a negative team can offer a counterplan involving the actions of social movements while critiquing state actors, using the critique to prove competition and serve as a reason to reject the plan. As this example illustrates, a critique functionally combines aspects of a counterplan and a disadvantage to create a distinct and very interesting type of argument.

Standard Format of a Critique

A. Link
B. Impact
C. Alternative

Debaters who are the subject of a critique can answer a critique in a manner similar to disadvantages and counterplans. For example, the affirmative can argue that the plan does not link to the critique, just as the affirmative would argue that the plan does not link to a disadvantage. Affirmative debaters can also argue that the critique does not outweigh the advantages of the plan or that the critique fails to solve the harms outlined by the affirmative.

Debaters can also raise objections to the use of critiques as a form of argument within a debate round. For example, many debaters argue that critiques are bad. They point to the lack of uniqueness and the fact that voting for a critique does not actually mean that the critique's alternative will occur. Many critiques offer utopian dreams with no real solvency for change, creating a whole new set of problems.

Arguing about Ethics

Debaters may also argue about the appropriate ethical frameworks that should be used to guide a debate discussion and ultimately determine the decision. While other ethical frameworks may be discussed during a debate round, the two most common ethical systems are consequentialism/utilitarianism and deontology.

Consequentialism/utilitarianism is a normative ethical theory based upon the work of philosophers like John Stuart Mill and Jeremy Bentham. They argued that the ethical decision is the one that maximizes utility, or obtains the most good for the greatest number, while minimizing bad consequences as much as possible. Within a debate round, this framework will focus the debate evaluation upon the consequences of action: the consequences (advantages/disadvantages) of voting for the plan, the consequences of voting for the status quo or the negative counterplan. The option that maximizes utility or good would be the option that wins the debate round.

Alternatively, debate can revolve around deontological concerns. **Deontology** is a normative ethical perspective that uses established rules to determine the morality of an action. It is most commonly associated with the philosophical work of Immanuel Kant. Within a debate round, deontology rejects the consideration of advantages, disadvantages, and any other consequences in favor of using clearly identifiable rules to evaluate the morality of an action.

For example, a deontological position may argue that going to war is evil because killing is wrong. This assessment of war is based upon the rule that all killing is murder and therefore wrong. Similarly, a deontological position may contend that state action is inherently evil. Therefore, any action undertaken by a state actor should be rejected, on face, regardless of any supposed advantages. Deontology has helped to ground the development of sophisticated critical arguments.

Evaluating Actions

The evaluation of actions is not limited to debate rounds. It is a part of life. Every day, you must make many different decisions involving the evaluation of actions, starting with the decision of whether and when to get out of bed. The evaluation of actions is personal and reflects an individual's view of the world. You may evaluate actions based upon your personal morality, choosing to engage in an action because you believe that it is the right or just or good thing to do. Alternatively, you may evaluate decisions based upon your evaluation of the likely consequences of the potential actions.

For example, two different people, A and B, may determine a need for transportation. Both need to be able to travel from home to college five days a week, so both consider purchasing a car. However, their evaluations look very different due to their personal views on how to evaluate actions. Person A may believe that ethics should guide the evaluation of the act of purchasing a new automobile. People concerned about polluting the environment with another combustion engine-driven automobile may feel obligated to investigate alternative actions, such as purchasing a bus pass or riding a bike. Alternatively, Person B is more inclined to consider consequences of actions, and thus would consider what a car purchase would yield. The advantages of a car purchase would include things like enhanced autonomy, the convenience of being able to travel freely, and the ability to consistently attend classes. However, there are also disadvantages of a car purchase, such as the lost money that must be spent to buy the car, the additional financial costs such as the purchase of insurance and a parking permit, and the purchases that have to be given up in order to have the money to buy the car. It is possible that Person A and Person B would arrive at the same decision not to purchase the car, but their evaluation of the action would look very different and they would arrive at the same conclusion through very different mental considerations.

Similarly, a debate round brings individuals with different personal views about how best to evaluate action into the same context. As a result, how they evaluate the posited action of the plan may become a point of contention. It is important for debaters to gain some familiarity with the ways that judges and opponents are likely to believe regarding the evaluation of action.

Problem-Solution

The **problem-solution framework** is a common technique. It involves focusing upon an established problem and then seeking the solution that is best to deal with that problem. The problem-solution framework tends to reject alternatives that do not involve some attempt at a solution: reliance upon the status quo just isn't good enough.

Comparative Advantage

Affirmatives can opt to argue that their plan has a **comparative advantage** over the status quo. Comparative advantage evaluations occur when two different actions will both produce positive or advantageous outcomes. As a result, the evaluation of the two options does not focus upon the negative consequences of one or both. Instead, the evaluation measures the comparative advantage enjoyed by one or the other.

Opportunity Cost

In policy debate, a counterplan is a negative argument presented as an opportunity cost of the affirmative plan. In economic theory, an **opportunity cost** presents the best alternative that must be foregone in order to adopt a posited action. Certainly, any action can have multiple competing alternative options. However, the opportunity cost is the one best alternative that must be given up if the posited action is selected. If the advantages of the posited action are more than the advantages of the action designated as the opportunity cost, then the posited action may be regarded as a good idea. On the other hand, if the advantages derived from the opportunity cost are better than that posited action, then the opportunity cost is the better choice and the posited action should not be adopted because adoption means giving up the opportunity to select the opportunity cost instead.

Similarly, if the counterplan is shown to be better than the plan and must be rejected in order to adopt the policy, then the policy judge will vote negative. Counterplans are an advanced debate concept and may initially seem confusing. Many students and even some coaches believe that a judge voting negative for a counterplan means that the judge is voting to adopt the negative's counterplan instead of the affirmative's plan. However, this explanation for the ballot decision is not entirely correct. Instead, the judge is voting that the opportunity cost of the plan is better than the plan itself. So, the plan should not be adopted. Then, if the judge were to evaluate the counterplan, opportunity cost analysis would support evaluating the counterplan against its own opportunity cost, which may or may not be the affirmative plan. Only the evaluation of the counterplan against its opportunity cost would yield a decision to adopt a counterplan and that evaluation falls outside of the scope of the typical policy round. Therefore, it is better for debaters to understand that a judge is not, by default, actually voting for a counterplan if the judge votes negative. The judge is simply voting not to adopt the affirmative plan.

Advantages and Disadvantages

Advantages are the beneficial consequences caused by the affirmative plan. Advantages may also be defined in terms of the negative's counterplan. **Disadvantages** are the negative consequences of the passage of the affirmative plan. Although disadvantages are typically viewed as a negative argument linking to the affirmative plan, it is also possible for the negative counterplan to trigger one or more disadvantages. Many debate rounds will come down to evaluating the impact of the advantages against the impact of the disadvantages. If the affirmative plan's advantages are greater than its disadvantages or the advantages of the counterplan, then the affirmative will win the round. Alternatively, the negative can win the round either by proving that the affirmative does more harm than good when compared to the status quo or to the negative's counterplan.

Conclusion

One on one debate requires debaters to think about why decisions should be undertaken. This mode of thought allows the debater to understand better how the judge evaluates the round. Debaters arguing the facts of a case or plan should be prepared to establish and debate the definition of resolutional terms and select criteria that communicate to the judge how the debater believes the round should be judged. Debaters should also prepare to evaluate the quality of evidence based upon factors such as the date of publication and the qualifications of the author of the piece of evidence.

Debating theory and ethics within a debate round is ultimately very difficult. Ethical considerations may be raised within both value debate and policy debate rounds. Debaters can choose to run critique arguments to challenge assumptions and draw the judge's attention to important structural problems. Debaters should also consider the use of different ethical frameworks, including deontology and consequentialism, to be used in conjunction with criteria as a way to evaluate rounds.

Key Terms

Advantage—the beneficial consequences caused by the plan or the counterplan.
Comparative Advantage—The measurement of the difference in positive gains, or advantages, between the affirmative plan and the status quo or negative counterplan.
Consequentialism/Utilitarianism—a normative ethical theory that argues the best option is the option that maximizes utility, or the greatest good for the greatest number.
Counterplan—A negative argument that serves as the opportunity cost of the plan, composed of four parts: counterplan text, conditionality, competition, and solvency.
Criteria—The standards upon which a decision will be made.
Critique—A disciplined method of analyzing oral or written discourse.
Disadvantage—A negative consequence caused by the passage of the affirmative's plan or the negative's counterplan.
Evidence—the statistics, facts, and opinion used to support a debater's argument.
Expert Evidence—Evidence written by someone with professional or educational credentials that make the author a qualified expert.
Opportunity Cost—The best option that must be foregone in order to undertake a particular action or decision.

Check Your Understanding

What is "criteria"?

What is "evidence"?

What is a "critique"?

Explain deontological

Explain problem-solution framework?

Explain comparative advantage framework?

Explain "opportunity cost"

A Sample One-on-One Debate Structure

Affirmative Constructive (AC)   4 min

The affirmative debater lays out a complete argument on behalf of the resolution at issue.

Cross Examination (CX)   2 min

The negative debater asks the affirmative debater questions.

Negative Constructive (NC)   4 min

The negative debater answers the affirmative's argument directly and offers their own objections to the affirmative's main claim.

Cross Examination (CX)   2 min

The negative debater asks the affirmative debater questions.

Affirmative Rebuttal (AR)   2 min

The affirmative debater does 3 things: offer a short overview, which explains

why the affirmative is correct, extend their argument from the affirmative constructive speech and answer the negative's objections to the main claim.

Negative Rebuttal (NR)   2 min

The negative debater does 3 things: offer a short overview which explains why the negative is correct, answer the remaining affirmative argument, and extend their own objections from the negative constructive.

CHAPTER
10 Team Debate

Chapter Objectives

Team debate gives interested debaters the option of not competing alone. Also known as two on two (2v2) debate, team debate is in many ways similar to one on one debate, except for one very important difference: instead of competing individually against another debater, you compete with a partner against a team of two other debaters. The presence of a partner considerably changes the structure of the round because speeches and preparation time must be shared. In addition, team debate also creates the opportunity for strategies not available in a one on one debate.

Within this chapter you will learn the most significant characteristics of team debate:

- Working with a partner
- Time management
- Strategic debate

The presence of a partner creates an interpersonal dynamic not found in one on one debate. Instead of acting independently within a round, a team debater must develop the skills needed to cooperate with a partner, sharing responsibility for the debate outcome. The structure of team debate allows both partners to deliver one constructive speech, one rebuttal, and to ask questions in one cross-examination. The affirmative team enjoys substantial control over the content of the debate by delivering the first and final speeches. Team debate also requires more precise time management skills, particularly due to the shared preparation time that must be carefully divided among the speeches offered by the partners.

Finally, team debate creates new strategic options not available in one on one debate. The negative enjoys the negative block. When labor is divided between the two negative speakers, the negative block helps to balance the affirmative's advantage of speaking first and last. The affirmative team can also vary speech assignment from the norm to help cover the weakness of one partner.

Working with a Partner

Team debate is a form of competitive debate that pits two sets of partnered debaters against each other. As with one on one debate, the side responsible for supporting the resolution is called the affirmative, or the aff. The opposing team is called the negative, or neg. Success in team debate requires the ability to collaborate with one's partner.

Interpersonal Issues

The presence of a partner changes the interpersonal dynamic of a debate. In one on one debate, the solo debater acts independently and enjoys total control over speech content. Without answering to anyone else (except, perhaps, one's coach before or after the round), the solo debater can decide what arguments to present and argue. As the debate progresses, the solo debater must make independent decisions about what arguments to extend and what to drop, where to focus the debate, and how to win the judge's ballot. A debater who wins can take credit for that victory and a debater who is defeated cannot pass the buck.

However, in team debate, one partner has to cooperate with another human being. The presence of a partner requires the debater not only to communicate with the judge and the opponent but also with an ally. Ideally, duties and responsibilities need to be negotiated prior to the start of a tournament. Then, the partners should work together during a round, each fulfilling pre-determined duties to support the goal of victory.

A partner immediately creates organizational challenges. For example, policy debate requires debaters to organize and present a considerable amount of evidence. If physical boxes are used to file and store that evidence, both partners must have access to that evidence and must also know how the files are organized in order to be able to pull that evidence quickly during a round. If only one debater knows the location of a particular file or piece of evidence, the other debater's ignorance can cause substantial delays in a debate round. In-round preparation time may be wasted or pivotal evidence forgotten unless both team members are organized and prepared.

Physical evidence is also an encumbrance that needs to be transported from room to room. Depending upon the tournament location, debaters may need to transport their evidence up stairs, to different buildings, and across parking lots. Unless accommodations are otherwise made, solo debaters can expect to be responsible for the transportation of their own evidence between debate rounds. In contrast, partners need to decide who is pushing the evidence, carrying the computers, or otherwise responsible for the team's shared equipment. One partner should never assume that the other will carry their tubs!

Team Debate Speeches

The presence of a partner creates a structural need for more speeches in the debate round. As a result, team debate rounds are roughly twice the length of one on one rounds in order to allow both members of both teams equal speaking time. There are four constructive speeches, four rebuttal speeches, and four cross-examination periods in a team debate round. The standard order of speeches for team debate is:

> first affirmative constructive (1AC),
> first negative constructive (1NC),
> second affirmative constructive (2AC),
> second negative constructive (2NC),
> first negative rebuttal (1NR),
> first affirmative rebuttal (1AR),
> second negative rebuttal (2NR) and
> second affirmative rebuttal (2AR).

A cross-examination period immediately follows each constructive.

This speech order means that the affirmative team speaks first and last, an important competitive advantage. The negative team, on the other hand, has a block of two back-to-back speeches (the 2NC and 1NR) that are divided only by a cross-examination. As with one on one debates, new arguments are intended to be limited to the content of the constructive speeches only.

The speeches for both sides are divided between the two partners equally. Each team member must deliver one constructive and one rebuttal. Typically, the **first affirmative speaker** will give the first affirmative constructive and the first affirmative rebuttal, while the **second affirmative speaker** will deliver the second affirmative constructive and the second affirmative rebuttal.

Similarly, the two negative speakers are also responsible for delivering two speeches each, one constructive and one rebuttal. The **first negative speaker** will give the first negative constructive and the first negative rebuttal. The **second negative speaker** will deliver the second negative constructive and the second negative rebuttal.

Team debate also creates a new dynamic for the cross-examination periods. As with solo debate, each constructive speech is followed by a cross-examination period that allows one debater to strategically question the opponent. In general, team debaters will divide their cross-examination duties so that each debater on each team asks the questions during one cross-examination.

A careful division of cross-examination labor allows a team to maximize preparation time. In general, the debater asking the questions is the member of the team who is not going to speak next. So, for example, the first affirmative speaker will question the first negative speaker after the first negative constructive. This strategy enables the second affirmative speaker to prepare for the upcoming second affirmative speech. The following chart details the general division of labor between team debate members.

Team Debate: The Division of Speech Labor

If the speaker is the . . .	Then the speaker is responsible for giving the . . .	And the speaker asks questions during the cross-examination of the . . .
First Affirmative	First Affirmative Constructive (1AC) First Affirmative Rebuttal (1AR)	1NC
Second Affirmative	Second Affirmative Constructive (2AC) Second Affirmative Rebuttal (2AR)	2NC
First Negative	First Negative Constructive (1NC) First Negative Rebuttal (1NR)	2AC
Second Negative	Second Negative Constructive (2NC) Second Negative Rebuttal (2NR)	1AC

As noted in a previous chapter, the cross-examination period is regarded by many judges as an informal part of the debate. Judges rarely flow the debaters' questions and answers. Some may not even pay attention. The answers given may be considered binding by the debaters but any arguments discussed within a cross-examination period must be raised during a following speech in order to ensure their placement on the flow sheet.

The informal nature of the cross-examination period offers team debaters some leeway on who is asking or answering questions. For example, the first negative speaker may ask a question that the first affirmative speaker cannot answer. Rather than allow a long silence that embarrasses the first affirmative, the second affirmative speaker can elect to help his partner by answering the negative debater's question. If the second affirmative offers a sufficient answer, the negative debater may then ask another question that the first affirmative speaker can answer. However, if the second negative speaker is unclear about the second affirmative speaker's answer, she may then ask for clarification. If this occurs, either affirmative debater can elect to answer the second negative speaker's question. As a result of this type of exchange, it is possible for all four of the round's debaters to participate in a single cross-examination period.

However, team debaters should be mindful of how their cross-examination conduct impacts the perception of the audience. Helping one's partner answer a difficult question is normal and part of being a team. However, constantly interrupting or correcting one's partner during cross-examination can significantly undermine the partner's credibility in the eyes of the judge. Such behavior may also make the more dominant debate partner appear bossy or unlikeable.

Therefore, as a general rule, it is a good idea to allow one debater to take lead on asking the recent speaker questions on the behalf of the team. Similarly, it is a good idea to allow one's partner to answer a question without aid. Interruptions should be reserved for situations where one's partner does not know an answer or gives an answer that is incorrect.

Furthermore, cross-examination should also be regarded as an important strategic resource. As a chart illustrated, the partner not responsible for asking questions is going to give the next speech. Therefore, cross-examination time offers additional preparation time that does not count against the team's total. If a debater is asking questions or arguing with the other team during cross-examination, that debater is not preparing for the next speech and preparation time that might otherwise be saved for a later speech may be required after the end of the cross-examination.

The Benefits of Partnership

Working with a partner also offers particular benefits. As an extracurricular activity, debate tends to draw like-minded individuals who share a love of critical thinking, conversation, and competitive success. Many debaters prefer the camaraderie that comes from having a debate partner. Debate partners spend hours together preparing arguments for tournaments. Debate partnerships often lead to friendships that continue long after the partners graduate and leave the activity. In fact, some debaters partner together in high school, graduate, and attend the same college so they can continue their debate partnership.

Of course, the substantial amount of time required to prepare for a debate does create some interpersonal pitfalls. If two debaters do not get along, their partnership may be strained and their competitive success may falter. Severe dislike may cause one or both debaters to quit the team or leave the activity entirely.

Within a debate round, the team also offers some practical advantages. A debate partner is an important reference. Debaters join the team with different life and educational experiences. They may have different majors and career aspirations. They may have different speech and delivery styles. Debate partnership provides the participants with the opportunity to interact with and learn from someone from a potentially very different socioeconomic, ethnic, and cultural background.

Debate partners help each other throughout the round. If one debater misses an argument raised by an opponent, that debater can ask the partner for help. Similarly, if one debater does not understand an argument, a quick question to a partner for clarification during the speech can avoid wasting time on the issue during cross-examination or prep time.

Debate partners also provide an important sounding board for round strategy. The second member of each team must give the final speech but the content of that speech is be shaped by the words conveyed by the speaker's partner. During the round, effective partners will talk about which arguments are succeeding and which are struggling. They will also talk about the strengths and weaknesses of the other team. These conversations, while brief, can substantially improve a team's chance at success.

Flowing a round is also much easier when two partners work together. Solo debaters have to preflow their speeches or rely upon memory to correct their flow after the completion of their speech. However, when participating in team debate, one partner can flow for the other partner. For example, if the debaters are flowing on paper, when the second affirmative speaker stands up to give the 2AC, the first affirmative speaker can take the paper flows of the partner. The first affirmative can flow the speech on her flow and then transfer the same arguments to her partner's flow.

This practice ensures that both speakers have a full record of all of the arguments raised during the speech. It also cuts down on prep time used since the debater who is about to speak does not have to pre-flow the speech in advance.

Debate partners can also help with time management issues. In one on one debate, a speaker must watch the clock while communicating arguments. In team debate, the speaker should still keep a timer but the speaker's partner should also have a timer. If the speaker falls behind on time, the partner can prompt the speaker to move on or even jump to a key argument. Many a debate round has been won thanks to one debater forcing a partner to address a key argument before the end of time. Conversely, if a speaker fails to answer an argument, both debaters are responsible for the oversight. Part of being a team means helping one's partner avoid major mistakes.

Time Management

Time management is an essential element of team debate. While this format doubles the number of speeches in the debate, it does not double the amount of preparation time allotted to each time. Furthermore, the two debaters must share the time in an effective manner. Once all of the team's preparation time is used up, any subsequent speeches must be delivered immediately after the end of the previous speech. Since good final speeches are essential to winning a round, debate partners must learn to use their preparation time as effectively as possible.

Instinctively, you may think that the debaters should share their preparation time evenly. For example, if each team is allotted 10 minutes total during a round, each member should get 5 minutes and that time should then be divided equally between the different speeches. While this may make intuitive sense, practice shows that successful debaters will tend to allot more preparation time to some speeches while giving very little, or even none, to others.

For the affirmative time, the total preparation time should really only be used for three speeches: the 2AC, the 1AR, and the 2AR. After all, the first affirmative speech begins the debate round. This speech is prepared long before the beginning of the round, before the debaters arrive at the tournament, and essentially has an unlimited supply of preparation time. The 1AC is also entirely scripted and should be timed. All that the first affirmative speaker has to do for that first speech is read it within time. Therefore, the affirmative team should not spend any preparation time until the 2AC.

The division of time among the three remaining affirmative speeches will vary from round to round, team to team. The 2AC will need time to pull evidence and prepare answers to the negative's initial arguments. However, many debaters will attempt to anticipate the arguments of their opponents and prepare **blocks** of organized answers prior to the round. A 2AC block will contain all of the answers to a given position, including any relevant evidence. If the negative team offers arguments not anticipated by the affirmative, the 2AC may require more preparation time.

Like the affirmative team, the negative only really divides preparation among three speeches: the 1NC, the 2NC, and the 2NR. The first negative rebuttal should never use any preparation time and any debater who takes preparation time for the 1NR is making a serious strategic error. The denial of any preparation time to the 1NR is due to the nature of the negative block. Once the two negative debaters divide their arguments for the block, the 1NR can focus upon preparing the speech while the 2NC and cross-examination are occurring. At the college level, a constructive speech lasts eight or nine minutes depending upon the organization, while a cross-examination is three minutes, which means that the 1NR has 11 to 12 minutes to prepare the rebuttal.

Often, the negative team knows the affirmative team's plan or position prior to the start of the round. For example, in team policy debate, an affirmative team will often disclose the text of their plan to the negative team in order to enable their pre-round preparation. This disclosure is done with the understanding that in the future, when the teams meet again but on opposite sides of the resolution, the other team will also disclose its plan. If a negative team knows the plan text prior to the round, that knowledge will enable substantial preparation for the 1NC to occur before the speeches begin. As a result, 1NC's will often be delivered with little to no preparation time used. Since the 1NR is prohibited from using preparation time, the second negative speaker will often enjoy the luxury of using all, or nearly all, of the team's preparation time for the 2NC and 2NR.

Always keep in mind that time is a precious resource in a debate. Arguments must be presented within allotted speech times and any argument made after the buzzer goes off may be ignored by the judges. In addition, once preparation time is used by a time, all subsequent speeches in a round must be given as soon as the opponent is done speaking. Therefore, it is essential that partners carefully manage their own use of time and that of their partners.

Strategic Debate

The addition of two more competitors to a one on one debate does not alter the substance of debate rounds and team debates may involve policy resolutions or values resolutions. Several team-oriented policy debate organizations exist at the university level, including the Cross-Examination Debate Association (CEDA) and the National Debate Tournament (NDT). The National Educational Debate Association (NEDA) is a team debate organization that debates one policy resolution and one values resolution every year. Team debate is also the standard in parliamentary debate programs. Parliamentary debate organizations, such as the National Parliamentary Debate Association (NPDA), the American Parliamentary Debate Association (APDA), and the World Universities Debating Championship (WUDC), organize team debate tournaments.

Nevertheless, the structural factors distinguishing team debate from one on one debate does create unique strategic opportunities. Debaters who recognize these features can improve their chances of tournament success by learning how to exploit these opportunities effectively. This section focuses upon two interesting strategic considerations of team debate: the negative block and the affirmative inside-outside speech order.

The Negative Block

One of the most important strategic elements of team debate is the division of labor within the **negative block,** which is the combination of the second negative constructive and the first negative rebuttal. The negative block is the only time in team debate where speakers from the same team speak consecutively. The affirmative team's speeches are always divided by a negative speech. The second negative constructive is directly followed not by the affirmative rebuttal but by the first negative rebuttal (the cross-examination does not really count, since it is an unflowed question period rather than a formal speech). This structure enables the negative team to put considerable pressure upon the first affirmative speaker, who is required to respond to arguments made within both speeches.

In order to maximize the advantage offered by the negative block, the members of the negative team must divide their labor. The key strategic consideration is to ensure that the two speeches do not overlap in content. However, one of the most common mistakes made by new debaters arguing the negative side of the debate is to fail to maximize the strategic advantage offered by the negative block. New debaters may fail to communicate their intent before the 2NC. If both speakers discuss the same disadvantage, for example, the affirmative's job becomes considerably easier in the first affirmative rebuttal.

In general, the negative division of labor will give the team's primary plan for winning the round to the second negative speaker for the 2NC, while the 1NR, the shorter of the two speeches, will be devoted to giving the team additional winning chances. For example, the second negative constructive may choose to discuss two disadvantages while the first negative rebuttal will discuss the case debate and the negative's topicality arguments. The second negative speaker would then need to decide what to argue in the 2NR, with preference given to the disadvantages.

Affirmative teams should generally understand that the arguments of the 2NC are likely to be arguments focused upon in the 2NR. After all, the second negative speaker will be more familiar with those arguments. Savvy affirmative speakers will often choose to focus considerable time in the 1AR on the 2NC's arguments for this reason. However, this choice could lead to the 1AR not adequately covering the 1NR's arguments. Therefore, strong first negative speakers will ensure that their speech contains arguments that, if not answered adequately, could also win the round for the negative team.

The Affirmative Inside-Outside Speech Assignment

Within team debate, both debaters are required to complete one constructive and one rebuttal speech each. As noted earlier, the affirmative team will typically assign one debater to deliver both the first affirmative constructive and the first affirmative rebuttal. The other member of the team will then be responsible for the second affirmative constructive and the second affirmative rebuttal. This assignment of speeches leads to the former debater being called the first affirmative speaker, while the latter is the second affirmative speaker.

However, most debate associations and tournaments do not have a formal rule requiring this division of labor. As a result, some teams adopt an **inside-outside debate order.** One speaker will deliver the first affirmative constructive and second affirmative rebuttal (the outsides), while the other will deliver the second affirmative constructive and the first affirmative rebuttal (the insides).

This strategy places tremendous pressure upon the debater delivering the inside speeches. The first affirmative rebuttal is largely regarded as the most difficult affirmative speech in the round due to the need to answer the negative block, and the second affirmative constructive is far more difficult than reading the prepared first affirmative constructive. As a result, affirmative teams using the inside-outside debate order are rare.

Nevertheless, some teams will use the inside-outside speech assignment when they are affirmative. This strategy works best for teams composed of two debaters of very unequal skill level. The stronger debater will complete the inside speeches. Since the first affirmative constructive is prepared and practiced before the debate round, the weaker debater then really only has to worry about delivering the second affirmative rebuttal. The stronger debater can further aid the weaker debater by using only a limited amount of preparation time. Then, most of the time can be devoted to the preparation of the round's final speech.

The decision to use the inside-outside order may impact judge perceptions of the ability of the team, as well as judge assignment of speaker points. Debaters who successfully complete the inside speeches are often rewarded by judges with higher speaker points. In contrast, the debater completing the outsides may receive lower points due to the reduced difficulty of the speech obligation.

Conclusion

Team debate provides competitors the opportunity to forge rewarding relationships with like-minded partners. Team debate expands the number of debaters from two to four. It also increases the length of round time and number of speeches. A team debate round contains four constructive speeches, four rebuttal speeches, and four cross-examinations. Each team debater is responsible for delivering one constructive speech, one rebuttal speech, and for asking questions in one cross-examination. Generally, the debater asking questions during cross-examination is the member of the team who is not speaking next.

Team debate is an interpersonal activity. Debate brings together similarly minded competitors and many partners enjoy life-long friendships. During competition, partners should help each other by sharing responsibility for timing speeches and gathering evidence. Successful time management is a priority because partners must share the in-round preparation time. The first affirmative constructive and first negative rebuttal should never require the use of preparation time.

Team debate also creates unique strategic opportunities for debaters. The negative team must divide labor for the negative block in order to maximize the pressure applied to the first affirmative rebuttal. When one partner is substantially stronger than the other, a team may engage in an inside-outside affirmative speech assignment in order to alleviate some of the speaking pressure for the weaker partner.

Key Terms

Block—Prepared list of answers to a specific argument.

First Affirmative—The first person to speak on the affirmative team, typically responsible for delivering the first affirmative constructive, the first affirmative rebuttal, and cross-examination of the first negative constructive.

First Negative—The first person to speak on the negative team, typically responsible for delivering the first negative constructive, the first negative rebuttal, and cross-examination of the second affirmative constructive.

Inside-Outside Affirmative Speech Assignment—Instead of the standard 1AC/1AR and 2AC/2AR speech assignments, the stronger or more experienced debater delivers the second affirmative constructive (2AC) and the first affirmative rebuttal (1AR), while the weaker or less experienced debater delivers the first affirmative constructive and the second affirmative rebuttal (1AC/2AR).

Negative Block—The sequence of speeches composed of the second negative constructive and the first negative rebuttal; the only time in the round where speakers from the same team speak consecutively.

Second Affirmative—The second person to speak on the affirmative team, typically responsible for delivering the second affirmative constructive, the second affirmative rebuttal, and cross-examination of the second negative constructive.

Second Negative—The second person to speak on the negative team, typically responsible for delivering the second negative constructive, the second negative rebuttal, and cross-examination of the first affirmative constructive.

Team Debate—a form of competitive debate that pits two sets of partnered debaters against each other.

Check Your Understanding

What are the three main characteristics of team debate?

1.

2.

3.

What interpersonal issues arise with team debate?

There are eight standard speeches for team debate. Name them and list their abbreviations.

1.

2.

3.

4.

5.

6.

7.

8.

When do cross-examinations occur?

Explain the "negative block"

Example: General Template for Affirmative case Based on Need

I. Introduction (some call it observation analysis)
   1. Resolution and stance:
   2. Statement of significance and impact.
   3. Define key terms or state that the terms will be defined operationally in the case. Don't forget to cite!
   4. Establish criteria on which you would like to be judged (policy is usually Cost Benefit).

II. Contention1: HARMS
   1. Harm #1 Claim:
      a. Data #1: Don't forget to cite all your evidence!
      b. Data #2:
      c. Data #3:
      d. Warrant:
      e. Reasoning:
   2. Harm #2 Claim:
      a. Data #1:
      b. Data #2:
      c. Data #3:
      d. Warrant:
      e. Reasoning:
   3. Harm #3 Claim:
      a. Data #1:
      b. Data #2:
      c. Data #3:
      d. Warrant:
      e. Reasoning:

III. Contention 2: INHERENCY
   a. Explain what is causing the harms.
   b. Explain what is keeping these harms from being solved or significantly reduced (structural- laws or attitudinal- cultural beliefs etc.)

IV. Contention 3: Plan
   a. Agency: What agency should oversee this plan?
   b. Mandates: What specifically is your plan for this?
   c. Enforcement: What would the punishments and rewards be for complying with your plan or failing to comply with your plan? This may be fines, imprisonment, removal of licensing etc....
   d. Funding: How are you planning to pay for this? Normal means is most commonly used.
   e. Addendum: This is where you discuss anything else your plan needs in order to work. You may need to remove a law- this is where you would mention that.

V. Contention 4: Solvency
   a. Explain and argue that your plan will work with examples and evidence. Don't forget to cite!
   b. Demonstrate the harms will be solved or significantly reduced with your plan
   c. Outline the advantages of your plan. You may want to use the same format as the harms.

VI. Reference page
   a. In alphabetical order
   b. Single spaced
   c. APA
   d. All sources used and cited in case including defintions.

A Sample Team Debate Structure

First Affirmative Constructive (1AC)   4 min

The first affirmative debater lays out a complete argument on behalf of the resolution at issue.

Cross Examination (CX)   2 min

The second negative debater asks the first affirmative debater questions.

First Negative Constructive (INC)   4 min

The first negative debater answers the affirmative's arguments directly and offers their own objections to the affirmative's main claim.

Cross Examination (CX)   2 min

The first affirmative debater asks the first negative debater questions.

Second Affirmative Constructive (2AC)   4 min

The second affirmative debater extends the first affirmative arguments and responds to the first negative's objections.

Cross Examination (CX)   2 min

The first negative debater asks the second affirmative debater questions.

Second Negative Constructive (2NC)   4 min

The second negative debater develops the debate by continuing to argue directly against the affirmative arguments and extending their partner's INC objections.

Cross Examination (CX)   2 min

The second affirmative debater asks the second negative debater questions.

First Negative Rebuttal (1NR)   2 min

The first negative debater develops the negative arguments not argued by the 2NC. A division of labor with their partner is crucial for effective use of this speech.

First Affirmative Rebuttal (1AR)   2 min

The first affirmative responds to 6 minutes of negative arguments in only 2 minutes, making the 1AR an exceptionally challenging speech.

Second Negative Rebuttal (2NR)   2 min

The second negative rebuttal should do 3 things: offer a short overview explaining why the negative is correct, focus on extending key negative objections, and answering crucial affirmative arguments.

Second Affirmative Rebuttal (2AR)   2 min

The second affirmative rebuttal should do 3 things: offer a short overview explaining why the affirmative is correct, answer the remaining negative objections, and extend crucial affirmative arguments.

Appendix: Fallacies of Logic

Now that you understand what an argument is and how to construct one correctly, you must understand how to recognize and avoid fallacies. A **fallacy** is an error in reasoning. This should not be confused with an error in facts—an error in facts refers to the data used to argue a point being inaccurate. Fallacies are specifically relevant to construction of an argument itself. A fallacy occurs when premises do not provide adequate support for the conclusion. A person "commits a fallacy" when an arguer attempts to get others to agree with their points by using poor reasoning. There are two different categories of fallacies, formal (deductive) and information (inductive).

What causes people to use fallacies in their arguments? It is usually because they are trying to appeal to the audience through emotion or the arguer themselves is emotional about the issue. Now, emotion in itself is not weak, in fact, to consider any argument that is emotional to be inherently fallacious would be just wrong. The point is you can use emotion in argumentation but not to the detriment of your logical argument. Conversely sometimes people use fallacious arguments on purpose. Purposefully used fallacious arguments are often crafted for a particular audience. You will see this frequently in political campaigns, several community groups, and even at your dining room table. And of course, sometimes fallacies are created out of pure mistake; unintentionally using fallacies is common but not an excuse. It is important you understand the different types of fallacies you may commit or witness others committing.

Formal Deductive Fallacies

In deductive logic you are held to a high standard. Your premises must both be true, and thus your conclusion is true. If either one of your premises is not true, then your conclusion cannot be true. In order for your argument to be valid, it must have true premises that lead to the acceptable conclusion. For example, the most commonly used example of a good deductive argument is:

> All men are mortal.
> Socrates is a man.
> Therefore, Socrates is mortal.

You see; if the two premises are true then it would be impossible for the conclusion not to be true. This is solid deductive logic. Any variation from this specifically concrete manner of arguing deductively may place you in the realm of faulty logic known as "committing a fallacy." Below you will find various types of fallacies commonly used in deductive reasoning.

Affirming the Consequent

The fallacy of **affirming the consequent** occurs when a premise associates one particular instance to an entire consequent or result. Affirming the consequent can be represented this way:

If P then Q
Q
Therefore, P

If Oprah owns a castle she is rich.
Oprah is rich.
Therefore, Oprah owns a castle

If Monty has an ear infection, then he has a fever
Monty has a fever
Therefore, Monty has an ear infection

Denying the Antecedent

The fallacy of **denying the antecedent** happens when the minor premise asserts that the antecedent does not obtain. A statement that has the "If P then Q" form is called a conditional statement. P is the antecedent and Q is the consequent of the conditional statement. Arguments that deny the antecedent are invalid because their conclusions do not necessarily follow from the premises. Denying the antecedent can be understood this way:

If P then Q
Not P
So, not Q

If you smoke cigarettes you will get lung cancer.
You don't smoke cigarettes.
Therefore, you won't get lung cancer.

If they are not sweating, touching their mouths, and fighting they are telling the truth.
They are sweating, touching their mouths, and fighting.
So, they are not telling the truth.

Equivocation

The fallacy of **equivocation** occurs when the arguer uses a word that has two different meanings in their arguments. For instance, the word "bank" could mean the place you keep your money and get loans. The word "bank" could also refer to the edge of a river.

The fraternity I want to rush has mostly kids who are rich.
My teacher told me I am rich in all the ways that matter in life.
I should rush and be admitted into that fraternity.

Division

The **division** fallacy occurs when the major premise of a deductive argument is concerned with characteristics that apply to a group as a whole, and cannot be "divided" and applied to specific cases.

Small businesses are shutting down at a rapid pace.
My mom owns a small business.
My mom is shutting down at rapid pace.

Accident

The accident fallacy is an interesting one, because just the name itself seems to imply that it was unintentionally illogical, when this is most likely not the case. The accident fallacy occurs when an arguer claims that a rule is applied to something to which it really doesn't apply. In other words, A is understood by the rule of Z. But, A doesn't actually fall under the rule of Z.

"Coach, you can't go in the locker room, only athletes are allowed in the locker room."

"You should not have shot that intruder, killing is bad."

False Dichotomy, also Known as the Either-Or Fallacy

Another common fallacy you see on TV, in your homes, and especially in political campaigns, is the false dichotomy or "either-or" fallacy. In the **false dichotomy** fallacy the arguer craftily misrepresents the number of options available to the audience. There are two options provided to an audience and usually one is clearly painted in a positive way and the alternative choice is awful, frightening, or completely unimaginable.

For example, you may have been told that, "If you don't vote Democrat, you vote Republican." This statement is not entirely true. There are more options out there, you could vote Libertarian, Independent, for the Peace and Freedom Party, and many others. There are more options, but the arguer doesn't want you to think of them, they merely want you to think about how much you would never vote Republican.

Just think back to your childhood for a moment, you were sitting down to eat your meal and your father placed a large scoop of peas next to your potatoes and chicken. You refused to eat them, and so he said, "You either eat your peas, or spend the rest of the night in your room." You see; either-or fallacies are everywhere!

"Either we increase the punishments for drug use and distribution or we accept defeat and legalize them."

Informal Inductive Fallacies

Inductive arguments are not held to quite as high of standards as deductive arguments. Solid inductive arguments provide support and evidence for their conclusions, but just because their premises are true does not exactly mean the conclusion is 100% true. Remember, all inductive arguments are by definition invalid arguments. Given the difference between the two types of reasoning there is a different standard of analysis as well. Logical errors in reasoning for inductive logic are usually measured on a scale of weak and strong argumentation. Herein you will find various fallacies that commonly occur in inductive logic.

Cherry Picking

To begin, **cherry picking** occurs when an individual points to a limited number of cases in order to support a particular conclusion, while also ignoring those cases that disprove the conclusion. Cherry picking may be intentional or accidental. Cherry picking is also known as the fallacy of incomplete evidence.

Cherry picking is a practice found within a wide range of real-life settings. As with many other forms of inductive reasoning, cherry picking is problematic and the extent of its problematic nature is dependent upon the actions of the arguer. For example, modern resume writing commonly employs cherry picking. In fact, this is an innocuous and even necessary practice. Employers don't want to know everything about the life of the candidate. So, the job applicant commonly cherry picks the most relevant and typically most positive things to share with the interviewer. However, most interviewers recognize resumes as one-sided and will ask questions in order to gather more information about a candidate.

For example, a resume may provide an individual's degree and place of education. However, the resume will exclude the fact that the applicant was recently fired for being intoxicated in the workplace. A resume will also highlight only personal strengths and ignore weaknesses. Cherry picking ultimately suppresses some of the truth in order to emphasize some of the truth that the arguer views as important to furthering the argument. The applicant will list good qualities and ignore bad qualities when writing a resume because the applicant wants to get the job.

Confirmation Bias

Confirmation bias is a form of cherry picking that describes how individuals tend to focus upon data that supports their pre-existing beliefs. Confirmation bias also leads individuals to interpret ambiguous results as confirming their existing beliefs, rather than acknowledging the ambiguity. Confirmation bias further means that individuals ignore research, data, and information that do not conform to their beliefs.

Confirmation bias is an especially common practice used to protect beliefs regarding deeply entrenched, emotional, or otherwise difficult-to-change views. Writers face a high risk of confirmation bias when preparing a written work. For example, a student preparing a paper on a controversial subject may spend all of her time collecting research that agrees with her views. She may then overlook or ignore those studies that disagree with her and the thesis of her paper. Similarly, a reporter investigating a court case may interview only witnesses and experts who agree with the reporter's legal assessment. In both cases, the result will be a written project influenced by the author's bias.

Bandwagon

Out of all the fallacies, the **bandwagon fallacy** causes the most irritation, and yet, can be highly successful on unsuspecting audiences. You will want to avoid this fallacy and all fallacies during your argumentation process because they reflect poorly on your credibility, call your ethics into consideration, and just look bad. Now, the bandwagon fallacy is simple, it asserts that because everyone else is doing it so should you. The bandwagon fallacy appeals to your sense of conformity, your desire to be similar, and the idea that we should be "keeping up." You will have seen this fallacy in action when your child comes to you begging for an iPad because "everyone else in my class has an iPad!" There are actually a few types of bandwagon fallacies, but they all basically argue the same way, which is by purposely constructing an argument that appeals the audience's desire to fit in or been seen as "normal."

Appeal to common belief bandwagon fallacy: "You need to understand and come to see what 7 out of 10 Americans already do, that legalizing marijuana is a good thing."

Appeal to common practice bandwagon fallacy: "You should buy your elementary-aged child a cell phone, most kids these days have cell phones and data plans."

Hasty Generalization

This is probably the most used fallacy in interpersonal, small group, and college argumentation classes. The **hasty generalization** fallacy is just as it sounds, it is a generalization that an arguer makes hastily (with little consideration). In direct terms, hasty generalizations are inferences drawn from insufficient data.

"A friend of mine signed up through the new health exchange website, no problem. The site is working great!"

"My uncle began smoking at age 15, smoked five packs a day, and lived until he was 83 years old. As a result, smoking isn't unhealthy like they say."

Slippery Slope

The next most common fallacy is called the "slippery slope." The **slippery slope** fallacy you have seen from the time you were small. You might have seen it in your local anti-drug campaigns, during parental reasoning, or while discussing politics. The slippery slope argument is basically what it sounds like, it asserts that if you take one tiny step in a certain direction you will fall head first in a downward tumble and that you will not be able to stop that momentum until you have hit the bottom of the hill.

The "fear tactic" is often used in conjunction with the slippery slope fallacy. Frequently, arguers assert that one small choice will just domino into a catastrophe and that catastrophe will be something greatly feared or universally avoided. The key to avoiding this fallacy is to make sure you have enough evidence to support the claim that if A, then B, if B then C, and if C then D, and that nothing will be able to stop that result. In short, the key to having a consequence argument not be a slippery slope fallacy is to ensure your data supports the claim totally.

"If they pass this waiting period on guns, they will do restrictions on assault rifles, and that will lead to gun bans everywhere. Stop the gun-grabbers now!"

"If you allow your child to watch a cartoon like Tom and Jerry, they will get hooked on violent video games, and then will do who knows what!"

False Cause or "Post hoc, ergo propter hoc"

In Latin, the false cause fallacy means, "after this, therefore because of this." Although that may sound confusing it is actually quite simple. What **false cause** fallacy means is that a false cause fallacy occurs when an arguer asserts that because one event followed another event the first event caused the second event. You can see why this is weak. Of course, there are occasions where one thing did cause another to occur right after, but more often, the cause of a given effect is not always due to whatever happened just before it.

This is a dangerous fallacy because it can be convincing to an audience who can see and understand the relationship between the two events, but hasn't really thought it through. Causality is difficult to demonstrate and control, so most often it is difficult to prove a cause and much easier to prove a correlation.

"Every time we won a game I wore one blue sock and one red sock. Therefore, if we want to keep winning I need to keep wearing my socks."

"Becky lost 14 lbs in one month. She started eating those yogurt-covered pretzels twice a week this month. Therefore yogurt-covered pretzels made Becky lose weight."

"Ice cream sales increase every June. The number of common colds lowers substantially every July. Therefore: higher ice cream consumption cures the common cold."

False Analogy, also Known as "Weak Analogy"

Analogies, as you have learned, are excellent forms of argumentation at times, but like any other argument they run the risk of becoming fallacious. The way to keep yourself from creating a false analogy is to be critical of your analogy. Make sure the things you are comparing are only different in very irrelevant ways.

An analogy-based argument presents the following idea:

X and Y are similar.
Since X has property A, Y has property A.

You know the analogy is fallacious if when you critique the analogy you find that there is a distinctive difference between the two that ultimately affects whether they both have property A.

"Education is like business, just as business is primarily concerned with overall profit, so should education."

General Informal Fallacies

The logical fallacies in this section are problems with informal reasoning. These are particularly troublesome because each has a germ of truth, each relies on shortcuts of thinking which can prove valuable at times, and each can be defended under certain circumstances. They are counted as logical fallacies because they do not, generally, hold up under careful argumentative scrutiny.

Appeals to Authority and False Authority

We have all encountered this argument. Just recently I was told that I must not support the new healthcare initiative because "Kim Kardashian says its going to cost a lot of money out of our pockets and let poor people have free insurance while the rest of us have to pay for it ourselves." This is an example of an argument based on a false authority. Who is Kim Kardashian? She is a reality TV star who rose to fame after a scandalous sex video went viral. Is this the definition of a credible authority on national healthcare reform? The answer is clearly a "no."

When we rely on the quotes and reasoning of others to substantiate our own arguments we must be critical of their character and expertise. If they are not experts and credible in the field they are discussing they are not usable in argumentation. Similarly, just because some has "Ph.D." after their name doesn't inherently make them credible either. There are many different credentials and each is relevant only depending on the topic at hand. For instance, let's say the authors of this book were asked to discuss a recent trend in argumentation and rhetoric and our evaluation of it. Given that the area is an area of our expertise, we would be considered credible experts. However, if we were asked to discuss the validity of the most recent physics theory, we would not be credible authorities on the subject.

Another way the **appeal to authority** fallacy is used is when someone is considered a credible expert in the field being discussed, but their perspective is offered as evidence that the claim is true instead of recognized as the opinion of one expert, which may not be representative of the entire field of experts. In other words, when citing or quoting an expert who agrees with your claim make sure your entire claim doesn't rest solely on the opinion of that one person, or you may be committing a fallacy of authority.

> *"Garcinia Cambogia is currently the best and most natural way to lose weight fast. Dr. Oz says Garcinia Cambogia improves mood, decreases appetite, and results in 4 lbs to 15 lbs of weight loss per month."*

Appeal to Ignorance

The **appeal to ignorance** fallacy occurs when an arguer asks the audience to create an inference based on a premise that is not proven, not provable, or lacks adequate support. Thus, the fallacy basically appeals to the ignorance of the audience. A common fallacy you might have heard is, " No one has proven that ghosts do not exist, therefore they do exist." The appeal is also frequently seen in politics when there has been insufficient research conducted.

In short, the appeal to ignorance argues that because something has not been proven false it is therefore true. It also may argue that something is false purely because it has not been proven to be true.

> *"Ghosts do not exist because no one has ever proven they exist."*

> *"Immunizations do not cause autism because research hasn't proven that they do."*

Red Herring

A **red herring** fallacy occurs when something irrelevant is presented in an attempt to divert the audience's attention from the actual issue at hand. This person will often make an argument that is basically unrelated to the topic, but just slightly connected in an attempt to get you thinking about that new (often emotion-evoking) issue and thus forget to argue the point at hand. They are primarily changing the topic.

> *"We agree that the issue of gays and lesbians having the right to marry is important. But, I also see that there are so many important issues to vote on and discuss right now that it's overwhelming and getting out of hand."*

Appeal to Fear

One of the most common types of fallacies you see on television is the "appeal to fear," which really means that someone is using a scare tactic. Using an appeal to fear means the arguer is triggering a fear response from the audience in order to get them to believe their claims. Humans are quite susceptible to fear tactics. For some reason it is just so much easier to accept a devastating possibility than to question the statistical likelihood of the idea.

> *"Recently three women have been attacked in their homes in various locations on the west side of town. Therefore, those of you living on the west side should stay locked indoors and make sure you have a defense device armed should you leave."*

Personal Attacks, also Known as "Ad Hominem"

An **ad hominem** fallacy occurs when an arguer attacks someone personally rather than the argument itself. Argumentation should always be directed at the logic and reasoning, not at the people progressing them, straying from this ideal results in a personal attack fallacy. You have endlessly endured these fallacies in political conversations. Former President of the United States Bill Clinton is still criticized for his affair with Monica Lewinsky when debates on his policies are debated. His womanizing ways are not what the debate is about, bringing up sexual history when discussing the effectiveness of his foreign policy qualifies as a personal attack, not a legitimate argument.

> *Jerome: "I gave you three reasons and three pieces of supporting evidence as to why abortion should be legal in the first trimester. I believe those abortions should remain legal."*

> *Skylar: "Of course you do, you're an atheist who doesn't believe in God, the commandments, and has no real appreciation for life."*

> *Jerome: "My being an atheist has nothing to do with this. My arguments were presented and evidence to back up my ideas given, that is what we are talking about."*

> *Skylar: "It doesn't matter what your reasoning is, if you are not religious you wouldn't understand."*

Hypocrite, also Known as "Ad Hominem Tu Quoque"

Ad hominem tu quoque is a kind of personal attack where the arguer doesn't just attack the person specifically at random, but does so because it points out an inconsistency in their arguments. The hypocrite fallacy is called such because it points out that person's arguments are inconsistent with their actions.

> *"Doing drugs like marijuana is bad and should be illegal. Marijuana is more harmful to your lungs than cigarette smoking. In fact, according to studies, smoking one marijuana joint is the same as smoking 3 to 24 cigarettes."*

> *Sam: "Do you smoke marijuana?"*

> *Beth: "Yes, on occasion."*

> *Sam: "You're a hypocrite!"*

Appeal to Tradition

An appeal to tradition fallacy occurs when it is argued that because something has been done in the past, is older, historical, or tradition it is therefore better or the best. This type of reasoning is problematic because age alone does not determine the legitimacy of something. Because people like their traditions they are likely to use this fallacy. We tend to stick with things we know because they are comfortable, safe, and predictable. But the idea that just because something is older or done more often in the past is inherently right is wrong and illogical.

> *"I have to believe in God. God and the bible have existed for centuries. The story of God and his teaching have been around for thousands of years so it must be true."*

> *"Traditionally the idea of marriage has been operationalized as a man and a woman committed to one another. It has always been that way and it should remain that way."*

Straw Man Fallacy

The **straw man** fallacy occurs when an arguer represents the opponent's position by presenting it as a weaker version than it really is, in an effort to more easily knock it down. Straw man fallacies are performed with a substitution of distorted, exaggerated, or misrepresented versions of the actual opposition argument.

> *"The congressman supports shutting down the nuclear weapons budget for one year, but I can't see why anyone would want to dismantle the United States' ability to defend itself."*

Self-Assessment: Logical Fallacies

1. Match the logical fallacy to the description
   - _____ false dichotomy
   - _____ hasty generalization
   - _____ denying the antecedent
   - _____ bandwagon
   - _____ affirming the consequent
   - _____ post hoc ergo propter hoc
   - _____ appeal to ignorance

   A. If P then Q. Q. Therefore P.
   B. I pitched a no-hitter after I wore my lucky underwear. I will wear those boxers for every game I pitch.
   C. Soylent is the new it food. Soylent must be really good stuff.
   D. You can't prove that ghosts don't exist, so they are real.
   E. Every atheist I have talked to is a lefty. No atheists are libertarians.
   F. Either you're for me or against me. You didn't vouch for me at the meeting, so you're against me.
   G. If P then Q. Not P. Therefore not Q.

2. Think of a logical fallacy that you heard or read recently. How did you or should you have handled it?

   _____

   _____

   _____

   _____

3. Slippery slope arguments are logical fallacies because the chances a sequence of possible causal events will all occur are small. Are slippery slope arguments always wrong? Explain.

   _____

   _____

   _____

   _____

Logic Games

Logic games are a standard way that someone's critical thinking abilities are tested. These games provide a description of a situation, constraints on possible ways to arrange the elements of the game are presented, and then questions are asked about possible ways to solve the logic game.

Logic games are a fun and challenging way to sharpen your critical thinking skills, get practice at drawing accurate inferences, and improve your ability to think logically.

How to solve a logic game

The 3 parts of every logic game

1. **The setup:** the paragraph description of the game at the beginning
2. **The rules:** the list of constraints on acceptable solutions of the game
3. **The questions:** the set of multiple-choice questions to answer

The 5 steps to solve logic games.

1. **Overview** [read the setup and only the setup for this step]
   a. Real world [what is this game describing in the real world?]
   b. Entities [identify the objects being manipulated in the game]
   c. Action [identify what is being done to the objects]
   d. Limits [do your counts, any limitations on action from just the setup?]

2. **Draw** [still just the setup, do a simple sketch of the game]
3. **Rules** [read the rules and note each in turn, building them into the sketch if you can]
4. **Deduction** [This is the key step. Combine rules together to come up with new constraints]
5. **Questions** [Look at the questions, one by one, for the first time.]

Game 1

At the track

Six racehorses - Rusty, Slowpoke, Turnip, Unbelievable, Vort3x, and Winning! will be assigned to six positions arranged in a straight line and numbered consecutively 1 through 6. The horses are assigned to the positions, one horse per position, according to the following conditions:

a. Rusty and Slowpoke are assigned to positions separated by exactly one position
b. Rusty and Unbelievable cannot be assigned to positions next to each other
c. Unbelievable must be assigned to a higher-numbered position than Turnip
d. Winning! must be assigned to position 3

Questions:

1. Which one of the following lists an acceptable assignment of horses to positions 1 through 6, respectively?
   a. Rusty, Slowpoke, Winning!, Turnip, Unbelievable, Vort3x
   b. Turnip, Rusty, Winning!, Slowpoke, Unbelievable, Vort3x
   c. Turnip, Unbelievable, Rusty, Winning!, Slowpoke, Vort3x
   d. Unbelievable, Vort3x, Winning!, Rusty, Turnip, Slowpoke
   e. Vort3x, Turnip, Winning!, Slowpoke, Unbelievable, Rusty

2. Which one of the following is a complete and accurate list of the positions any one of which can be the position to which Rusty is assigned?
   a. 1,2
   b. 2,3
   c. 2,4
   d. 2,4,5
   e. 2,4,6

3. Which of the following CANNOT be true?
   a. Rusty is in 2
   b. Slowpoke is in 2
   c. Turnip is in 1
   d. Turnip is in 5
   e. Vort3x is in 2

Game 2

At The Fair

A train ride at the Kern County Fair has exactly six cars, numbered 1 to 6 from front to back. Six children will get into those six cars, one child per car. The six children are Alan, Betty, Charlotte, David, Ellen, and Frank.

- a. Alan must be in either the first or the last car.
- b. Charlotte and David must be in adjacent cars.
- c. Frank has to sit further back in the train than Ellen sits.

Questions:

1. Ellen CANNOT be in which of these cars?
   - a. car 1
   - b. car 2
   - c. car 3
   - d. car 5
   - e. car 6

2. If Betty and Charlotte sit in adjacent cars and David is in the last car, then Frank has to sit in which car?
   - a. car 1
   - b. car 2
   - c. car 3
   - d. car 4
   - e. car 5

3. If David is in the front car, which of these CANNOT be the case?
   - a. Allan is in car 6.
   - b. Betty is in car 3.
   - c. Charlotte is in car 2.
   - d. Ellen is in car 5.
   - e. Frank is in car 4.

Game 3

Send in the Clowns

Your circus employs seven clowns, Felix, Gordon, Iris, Julia, Karl, Laura, and Marcia. Clown Law requires them to perform in the Big Tent one at a time, in order, from first to seventh. Each clown is either a happy clown or a sad clown. The following conditions apply:

a. The clown performing first is a happy clown and the clown performing last is a sad clown.
b. Both Felix and Karl perform before Marcia performs.
c. Laura performs before Gordon performs.
d. Julia performs second.
e. At least 2 happy clowns perform after Marcia's performance.

Questions:

1. Which of the following is an acceptable order of clown performances?

    a. Felix, Iris, Karl, Marcia, Julia, Laura, Gordon
    b. Felix, Julia, Karl, Marcia, Gordon, Iris, Laura
    c. Felix, Julia, Laura, Marcia, Iris, Karl, Gordon
    d. Karl, Julia, Felix, Marcia, Laura, Iris, Gordon
    e. Karl, Julia, Marcia, Laura, Felix, Gordon, Iris

2. Which of the following must be true?

    a. Felix is a happy clown.
    b. Julia is a sad clown.
    c. Karl is a sad clown.
    d. Laura is a happy clown.
    e. Marcia is a happy clown.

3. If exactly four happy clowns perform and NO sad clown's performance immediately follows another sad clown's performance, then each of the following must be true, EXCEPT?

    a. Felix is a happy clown.
    b. Gordon is a sad clown.
    c. Julia is a sad clown.
    d. Karl is a happy clown.
    e. Marcia is a sad clown.

Game 4

Holiday Shopping

A holiday shopper will purchase exactly five video games at a certain store. The shopper will select from seven different video games - Food Fight 4, Grossout, Higher, Jewel Quest, Knights 7, Losing!, and Mortality. No other games may be purchased. The shopper will select video games according to the following conditions:

a. Either Jewel Quest or Mortality will be purchased, but both cannot be purchased.
b. If Losing! is purchased, then Higher must be purchased.
c. If Grossout is purchased, then Jewel Quest cannot be purchased.

Questions:

1. If Food Fight 4, Grossout, and Knights 7 are three of the video games purchased by the shopper, which of the following must be the other two video games purchased?

   a. Higher and Jewel Quest
   b. Higher and Losing!
   c. Higher and Mortality
   d. Jewel Quest and Losing!
   e. Losing! and Mortality

2. If Grossout is purchased, which of the following must also be purchased?

   a. Food Fight 4
   b. Jewel Quest
   c. Knights 7
   d. Losing!
   e. Mortality

3. Which of the following is an acceptable combination of video games purchased by the shopper?

   a. Food Fight 4, Grossout, Higher, Knights 7, Losing!
   b. Food Fight 4, Grossout, Knights 7, Losing!, Mortality
   c. Food Fight 4, Higher, Knights 7, Losing!, Mortality
   d. Grossout, Higher, Jewel Quest, Knights 7, Losing!
   e. Higher, Jewel Quest, Knights 7, Losing!, Mortality

Game 5

The Accidental Tourist

While on vacation, a tourist will visit six cities: Rome, Stockholm, Trieste, Vienna, Warsaw, and Xiamen. The tourist visits the cities one after another, according to the following rules:

 a. Rome is visited after Warsaw and before Xiamen.
 b. Vienna is visited immediately after Warsaw.
 c. Stockholm is not visited immediately before or immediately after Trieste.

Questions:

1. Which of the following must be true?

 a. Either Stockholm or Trieste is visited fourth.
 b. Either Stockholm or Trieste is visited fifth.
 c. Either Trieste or Warsaw is visited first.
 d. Either Trieste or Xiamen is visited sixth.
 e. Either Vienna or Warsaw is visited second.

2. If Stockholm is visited third, which of the following is impossible?

 a. Rome is visited fourth.
 b. Rome is visited fifth.
 c. Trieste is visited fifth.
 d. Warsaw is visited first.
 e. Xiamen is visited sixth.

3. Which of the following is an acceptable order, from first to sixth, that cities could be visited?

 a. Trieste, Vienna, Warsaw, Stockholm, Rome, Xiamen
 b. Rome, Warsaw, Vienna, Stockholm, Xiamen, Trieste
 c. Warsaw, Vienna, Rome, Trieste, Xiamen, Stockholm
 d. Warsaw, Vienna, Rome, Xiamen, Trieste, Stockholm
 e. Xiamen, Warsaw, Vienna, Trieste, Rome, Stockholm

Game 6

Philosophers In The Wilderness

The chairperson of the Wilderness Club must choose two 2-person canoeing teams for an upcoming expedition. The club members available for the expedition are Chomsky, Dummett, and Eluard, who are experienced canoeists while Quine, Russell, Spinoza, and Tarski are novices.

- a.   At least one experienced canoeist must be in each canoe on the expedition.
- b.   Dummett and Russell will be chosen only if the two are in different canoes.
- c.   If either Chomsky or Spinoza is chosen, the other must also be chosen.
- d.   Spinoza will not be chosen if Tarski is chosen.
- e.   Eluard will not be chosen if Quine is chosen.

Questions:

1.   Which of the following is NOT an acceptable selection for the canoe trip?

- a.   canoe 1: Dummett and Quine
      canoe 2: Chomsky and Spinoza
- b.   canoe 1: Chomsky and Eluard
      canoe 2: Russell and Spinoza
- c.   canoe 1: Dummett and Chomsky
      canoe 2: Eluard and Spinoza
- d.   canoe 1: Eluard and Russell
      canoe 2: Dummett and Tarski
- e.   canoe 1: Chomsky and Spinoza
      canoe 2: Eluard and Dummett

2.   Which of the following must be true?

- a.   Chomsky and Quine cannot both be chosen
- b.   Dummett and Spinoza cannot both be chosen
- c.   Tarski and Chomsky cannot both be chosen
- d.   If Eluard is chosen, Russell cannot be chosen
- e.   If Tarski is chosen, Spinoza must also be chosen

3.   If Quine is chosen for Canoe 1, who must be in Canoe 2?

- a.   Eluard
- b.   Chomsky
- c.   Russell
- d.   Spinoza
- e.   Dummett

Game 7

Fishy, Fishy, Fishy.

A pet storeowner has put nine animals into three different tanks - a blue tank, a red tank, and a yellow tank. The nine animals are four newts, two crabs, a goldfish, and two angelfish.

   a. There is at least one newt in each tank.
   b. The two crabs are not in the same tank.
   c. The goldfish is in a tank that contains at least one angelfish.
   d. The goldfish is not in the yellow tank.

Questions:

1. If the goldfish is in the blue tank, and if all three tanks contain the same number of animals, all of the following must be true except:

   a. The yellow tank contains exactly one crab.
   b. The red tank contains exactly one angelfish.
   c. The blue tank contains exactly one angelfish.
   d. The red tank contains exactly one crab.
   e. The blue tank contains exactly one newt.

2. Which of the following could be a complete and accurate list of the contents of the blue tank?

   a. one newt, two crabs, one angelfish
   b. two newts, one goldfish, one crab
   c. one newt, one crab, one goldfish, one angelfish
   d. one goldfish, one angelfish
   e. three newts, one crab, one goldfish, one angelfish

3. If the red tank contains no angelfish and no crabs, which of the following must be true?

   a. The goldfish is in the blue tank.
   b. Two newts are in the red tank.
   c. Both angelfish are in the yellow tank.
   d. The blue tank contains exactly four animals.
   e. The yellow tank contains exactly two animals.

Game 8

At The ZOO

A zoo curator is selecting animals to import for the zoo's annual summer exhibit. Exactly one male and one female of each of the following types of animal are available: hippo, llama, monkey, ostrich, panther. The following restrictions apply:

    a.   If no panthers are selected, then both ostriches must be selected.
    b.   A male panther cannot be selected unless a female llama is selected.
    c.   If a male monkey is selected, then neither a female ostrich nor a female panther maybe selected.
    d.   At least one hippo must be selected.

Questions:

1. Which one of the following is an acceptable selection of animals for the exhibit?
    a.   female hippo, female monkey, male monkey, male ostrich, male panther.
    b.   female hippo, male llama, female monkey, female ostrich, male ostrich.
    c.   male hippo, female llama, male llama, female monkey, female ostrich.
    d.   male hippo, female llama, male monkey, female panther, male panther.
    e.   female llama, male llama, male monkey, female ostrich, male panther.

2. Which one of the following must be false?
    a.   Both a female hippo and male panther are selected.
    b.   Both a male monkey and a female llama are selected
    c.   Both a female ostrich and a male hippo are selected.
    d.   All of the animals selected are female.
    e.   All of the animals selected are male.

3. If a male monkey is selected, then which one of the following animals must also be selected?
    a.   female hippo
    b.   male hippo
    c.   female llama
    d.   female monkey
    e.   male ostrich

Game 9

Oh-Oh! Budget Cuts!

A university library budget committee must reduce exactly five of eight areas of expenditure — G, L, M, N, P, R, S, and W—in accordance with the following conditions:

    a.   If both G and S are reduced, W is also reduced.
    b.   If N is reduced, neither R nor S is reduced.
    c.   If P is reduced, L is not reduced.
    d.   Of the three areas L, M, and R, exactly two are reduced.

Questions:

1. Which one of the following could be a complete and accurate list of the areas reduced?

    a.   G, L, M, N, W
    b.   G, L, M, P, W
    c.   G, M, N, R, W
    d.   G, M, P, R, S
    e.   L, M, R, S, W

2. If W is reduced, which one of the following could be a complete and accurate list of the four other areas to be reduced?

    a.   G, M, P, S
    b.   L, M, N, R
    c.   L, M, P, S
    d.   M, N, P, S
    e.   M, P, R, S

3. If P is reduced, which one of the following is a pair of areas both of which must be reduced?

    a.   G, M
    b.   M,R
    c.   N, R
    d.   R,S
    e.   S,W

4. If both L and S are reduced, which one of the following could be a pair of areas both of which are reduced?

    a. G,M
    b. G,P
    c. N,R
    d. N,W
    e. P,S

Name: _____   Class: _____

Game 10

Look At The Pretty Beads.

A jeweler makes a single strand of beads by threading onto a string in a single direction from a clasp a series of solid colored beads. Each bead is either green, orange, purple, red, or yellow. The resulting strand satisfies the following specifications:

    a.   If a purple bead is adjacent to a yellow bead, any bead that immediately follows and any bead that immediately precedes that pair must be red.

    b.   Any pair of beads adjacent to each other that are the same color as each other must be green.

    c.   No orange bead can be adjacent to any red bead.

    d.   Any portion of the strand containing eight consecutive beads must include at least one bead of each color.

Questions:

1.   If the strand has exactly eight beads, which one of the following is an acceptable order, starting from the clasp, for the eight beads?

    a.   green, red, purple, yellow, red, orange, green, purple
    b.   orange, yellow, red, red, yellow, purple, red, green
    c.   purple, yellow, red, green, green, orange, yellow, orange
    d.   red, orange, red, yellow, purple, green, yellow, green
    e.   red, yellow, purple, red, green, red, green, green

2.   If an orange bead is the fourth bead from the clasp, which one of the following is a pair that could be the second and third beads, respectively?

    a.   green, orange
    b.   green, red
    c.   purple, purple
    d.   yellow, green
    e.   yellow, purple

3.   If on an eight-bead strand the second, third, and fourth beads from the clasp are red, green, and yellow, respectively, and the sixth and seventh beads are purple and red, respectively, then which one of the following must be true?

    a.   The first bead is purple.
    b.   The fifth bead is green.
    c.   The fifth bead is orange.
    d.   The eighth bead is orange.
    e.   The eighth bead is yellow.